PRASE FOR T[
MARKETING M

CW00727629

"With both his heart and his head, David has meticulously and methodically dissected the issues facing today's marketing professionals around the world.

In this 'survival handbook' for today's marketing professionals serious about their professional development, provocative manifestos such as 'What the hell *is* a marketer?' and 'Marketing, finance and accountants unite!', make the compelling case as to why a change is needed in the way marketing professionals are supported, recognized and developed around the world in order that they can become more knowledgeable, capable and promotable.

Indeed, we believe *The Marketing Manifesto* is such an important contribution to the body of marketing knowledge that we encourage all members of Global Marketing Network to read it! David reminds us all why we came into the marketing profession, the importance of marketing in today's organizations, and the duties and responsibilities we all have in creating a stronger and more supportive profession than the one we all entered. As the worldwide professional body for marketing, committed to raising standards in marketing practice, we wholeheartedly encourage all those associated with the development of the marketing profession, whether they are scholars or industry practitioners, to read it, discuss it and take action!"

Darrell Kofkin, CEO, Global Marketing Network

"This book is unique in its approach to marketing and I very much welcome it as a much-needed alternative to many current traditional structures.

I particularly welcome it because it addresses several dimensions that I have grappled with over the last decade or so.

Firstly, as a marketer I always wanted the marketing profession to try and develop both a professional and responsible approach to marketing. This led me to work, with the support of colleagues such as David, to develop not only the national occupational standards for the professional marketer and sales person but also allow marketing to reach the 'non-marketer' businessman through the development of non-specialist occupational standards that aimed to support SME organizations without a specialist marketer.

We finally developed occupational standards for social marketing to highlight the social benefits of marketing which, for too long, has been associated with cut-throat irresponsible competition. In this respect David's book addresses the contradictions we had to face throughout our work but also the challenges we were confronted with by rigid perspectives towards marketing from so-called 'guardians of the faith'. David's approach also aims to put marketing back in the hands of the marketers and not be rigidly constrained by organizations that may not serve best the discipline since they are already ruled by their state of *fait accompli*.

Secondly, as an educationist I have always worked hard to understand the obstacles that prevented some learners from mastering better their fields of study compared to others. This book will help the marketing learner, and teacher, to unravel several recurring issues to eventually enable a deeper level of understanding of their subject matter. Accordingly, I will add the arguments and approach offered in the book to my teaching armamentarium.

Thirdly, as a psychologist, I have always tried to understand conflicts to support their healthier resolutions. In the process, I developed a methodology based on a new quantitative method known as fuzzy logic. I think David's approach which uses the core conflict approach, is not dissimilar to this method, and is a breath of fresh air as it would help marketers challenge 'received wisdom' to help resolve the apparent contradictions.

Clearly part of the aim of the book is not so much to give an apology for the 'greatness of marketing', nor is it to diagnose or provide final answers to the apparent issues and associated contradictions. Rather in my view the biggest advantage of this book is that it challenges and helps unsettle the readers and in the process gets them to question over-learnt platitudes about marketing so that underpinning assumptions are uncovered and, ultimately, core issues revealed. This in turn would make the challenges assume the urgency of a call to arms.

Consequently, I unreservedly recommend the use of this book by anybody who wants to get to see marketing with warts and all which, at the same time, becomes the basis for future resolutions and reconciliations."

Dr Chahid Fourali FCIM, FRSA, Founder and Past Leader of the
Marketing and Sales Standards Setting Body

"Marketing has always been the misunderstood cousin of the Finance Department, but the art of marketing is increasingly becoming a measurable science which certainly helps. But that's not enough, marketing success also depends heavily on building relationships across the business and particularly getting Marketing and Finance to work together and speak the same business language with a customer focus.

The Marketing Manifesto demonstrates through 15 manifestos exactly how to get the most out of Marketing. Marketers need to be change agents, for example by putting the customer first, treating marketing as a pan company process, and keeping ahead of the curve in predicting future needs as an agent for the customer. The book logically tests assumptions and then takes us through necessary changes and the taking of brave steps towards achievement. A thoroughly good read and useful reference for marketers and managers in the business challenges that lie ahead."

Ray Perry, Executive Director of Brand, Profile and Marketing,
Chartered Institute of Management Accountants (CIMA)

"It's fantastic. It was just what I needed. Refreshing, revitalizing and inspirational."

Louise Watkins, Marketing and Inside Sales Manager, Microsoft

The Marketing Manifesto

The Marketing Manifesto

David James Hood

KoganPage

LONDON PHILADELPHIA NEW DELHI

First published in Great Britain and the United States in 2013 by Kogan Page Limited

120 Pentonville Road	1518 Walnut Street, Suite 1100	4737/23 Ansari Road
London N1 9JN	Philadelphia PA 19102	Daryaganj
United Kingdom	USA	New Delhi 110002
www.koganpage.com		India

© David James Hood, 2013

ISBN   978 0 7494 6852 1
E-ISBN   978 0 7494 6853 8

British Library Cataloguing-in-Publication Data

A CIP record for this book is available from the British Library

Library of Congress Cataloging-in-Publication Data

Hood, David J.
   The marketing manifesto / David Hood.
      p. cm.
   Includes index.
      ISBN 978-0-7494-6852-1 – ISBN 978-0-7494-6853-8 (ebook)   1. Marketing.   2. Customer relations.   I. Title.
   HF5415.H7545 2013
   658.8–dc23
                                                                          2012039955

Typeset by Graphicraft Limited, Hong Kong
Printed and bound in India by Replika Press Pvt Ltd

To my soulmate Eleanor, gràdh geal mo chridh
and 'shining light' for her love, inspiration and spirit,
who along with my delightful daughters Laura and
Jennifer give me a sense of privilege and purpose;
my late mother Irene for encouraging me to always ask
questions; and good friends and family who ensure
my feet are kept firmly on the ground by offering
their welcome and invigorating probity.

CONTENTS

FOREWORD

David is very enthusiastic about changing the face of Marketing... as we know it! He is also very knowledgeable about the societal, industry and technological trends and key factors that will impinge a tremendous degree of change in the way companies perform their marketing function.

The plethora of the new marketing manifesto is vast and challenging! From re-humanization and marketing futurecast to marketing misanthropy and repugnance. David's book brings a breath of fresh air to a beneficial structure of marketing thinking that has evolved very little since its inception as a management discipline.

David's inquisitive mind percolates throughout the text. Many challenging questions are raised and visionary, positive insights are brought forward. The methodological reasoning based on market sensing is patently visible. The priority challenges and opportunities for marketing are encapsulated in the mini-manifestos. After the market sensing stage, David reinforces the 'what' and the 'how' to change.

The book contains very strong statements, which call for a concentrated analytical discussion and reasoning. David's discourse builds up on dissecting contradictions, oxymorons and theoretical constructs that are proved to be facing a 'vacuum'... David does this very well by testing assumptions and propositions. The text is full of self-reflection passages and action hints.

His incitement to bravery is also to be commended. David questions the very essence of the profession. The phraseology is great, for example, 'tactical automatons'. David underpins contradictions and confronts established beliefs. He has refreshing ideas about process based Marketing Management (PBM2).

The content of the book is well absorbed thanks to its reader-friendly format. I am very pleased that David has dedicated one Manifesto to Marketing Futurecast. The concept of Marketing as a consumer agency is visible throughout the text. The prose of ideology flows like a system of signs that are designed to transform the reader's mind. I applaud David's strong statements about corporate misalignment and the no-change/no-future driven marketing recruitment. 'Playing safe' is definitely not an attitude that David Hood cherishes!

A lot of thought experimentation is distilled when unfolding each manifesto. The systematic approach of an organization is also another dominant; human sensing is another constant. The author dissects well the core principles of customer or consumer centricity. The diagnosis of Marketing Misanthropy (Manifesto 7) is profound and totally accurate.

Clearly, the collection of Hood's Manifestos is leading towards the vision of Common Sense Marketing (CSM). The critical fabric and make-up of marketing has to be altered, and this is the essential element, but its terminology and symbology probably has to be changed as well. The text is also replenished with vibrant proverbs and sayings, which instinctively substantiate the imparting of the axioms or postulates to the reader.

It has been 50 years since the inception of marketing as a management discipline; the philosophy, practice and the profession needs this new Marketing Manifesto. The stance of humanity, human-to-human interaction, and human-to-human dialogue has many implications for managing a company's landscape.

The book is full of relevant, challenging and mind-stretching propositions. It is a very thought provoking text designed to alter cognition and behaviour. Consumer-generated marketing (CGM) and proscription are also important markers within the structural reasoning.

David also adopts a comical and self-critiquing stance to illustrate the current state of thinking (eg, the 17Ps)... the sum of exposed marketing 'peccadilloes' is coherent. This book requires the reader to display some mental agility. This book is not for the faint of heart!

David's book will contribute to the much-needed shake-up and turnaround of marketing thinking. It is not only the change that is important, but also what lies behind the change.

The intertwining of ideas and cross-fertilization of concepts between manifestos is a major reinforcer for radical thinking. As David says... your choice! David unfolds many marketing paradoxes and oxymorons.

This book reflects that evolutionary marketing is here to stay. Philosophical insights and 'mind-stretching' provocations – they are the focus of this text.

Ponder and change!

Professor Luiz Moutinho
Foundation Chair of Marketing, University of Glasgow

ACKNOWLEDGEMENTS

Thanks go to my friend and colleague Professor Luiz Moutinho, Chair of Marketing at the University of Glasgow; not only for his kind Foreword and further contribution to this publication but for his inspiring and enduring indefatigability in prising open marketing's Pandora's Box, providing provocation to the senses and revealing an enlightened path ahead for us all as the creator of *Marketing Futurecast*®.

My thanks also extend to Microsoft and Darrell Kofkin, CEO, and Ian Derbyshire, Chair of the Global Marketing Network for sharing, spreading and indeed augmenting the vision, and now the journey, to make marketing a more precise, productive, principled and powerful practice.

Introduction

Marketing... a profession and business subject that is urgently in need of an immediate evolution, or radical revolution – indeed it is arguably undergoing a revolution in large part WITHOUT us marketers. What is offered here is a means to both fundamentally and powerfully address some outstanding crucial core issues, to allow for greater immediate improvements to your personal and corporate prowess at marketing.

I am certain that you also feel as though a change is more than overdue. It – both marketing and its practice – is seriously underperforming in terms of its status and place as a strategic business activity, and this is consequently lowering its potential to be the prime driver of value for the business. Marketing can and should be the primary, defining potent and perfect agent for competitive sustainability and long term advantage.

Why focus effort on some less important, small symptoms or nuisances, when you can set about fixing the greater concerns and realizing the superior opportunities facing you as a marketer?

DAVID JAMES HOOD

Indeed, it should additionally be an agent for *YOU*

Marketing – and your ability to utilize it – should extend and sharpen your personal prowess and that of your organization well beyond what any other business practice or process can. It should enable and empower you to make the best decisions possible – based on the ability to unquestionably and incontrovertibly identify and deliver what the customer needs and wants, and deliver it most profitably.

Has marketing achieved this satisfactorily, never mind admirably? I would assert that it has not. Far from it.

It certainly has not lived up to the expectation, aspiration and role. In addition, those who purport to develop and aid our profession have not yet managed to give it the leadership role, status and defining professional proficiency, it deserves. Therein lies the opportunity for you...

I have endeavoured in this book to examine marketing and the marketer, both from a 'scientific' viewpoint as someone keen to examine and find some form and robustness within marketing and also as a true devotee of what we marketing practitioners wish it *could and should be* and to help realize our vision for it.

Marketing surely has to be a robust, virtuous paradigm and process that finally comes of age; that not only steadfastly leads the organization and manages its obvious and not-so-obvious 'deliverables' but could and should shake off the predominant perception that it is little more than an art or alchemy that deceives and browbeats the prospect into becoming a customer.

Additionally, although marketing is 'blessed' with interesting and invigorating choices and offers a whole armoury of 'marketing mix' elements at our disposal, we are additionally predisposed to maintain an unhealthy addiction for the headlong dash to the new, the quick fix, fad or tactic coming just around the corner. We marketers have also accepted and nourished a lamentably glib and pathological faith in the simplistic case study or 'one size fits all' approach and the correspondingly glib transferable new stratagem.

What I intend here is to illustrate and tackle some major outstanding issues that we should address immediately if we really are to excel personally and corporately, in marketing.

As marketers, we are keen to develop our profession and our organization's capabilities in marketing, but we shouldn't overlook *what really needs to be done first*. For example, as marketers we need to address the obvious absence of a robust and established prioritizing methodology to ensure whatever we do – a stratagem, process, tactic or technology employed – is based on what we need to do now, to prevent us simply trying to adhere to the frenzied conventions of the new, or bind ourselves with the fossilized chains of the past.

Marketing is an uncertain art, and needs to radically evolve – or revolutionize – to meet the expectations of its practitioners and those who place their faith in the marketer. 'Budgets' – or marketing *spend* as most see it – must be 'well spent'; prospects, consumers and customers must flow in at a suitable rate and be secured; revenue must always be on tap as we rise to the challenge of creating sustainable competitive advantage in uncertain times.

Marketing is the process where the heart, pulse and power of the business should be. However, we need to be WORTHY of that position as custodians of marketing and competitiveness.

Can we do this? Can we give ourselves the means to resolve deep challenges and opportunities and set us on course for a fulfilling role and organizational efficacy that has thus far eluded us? Can we update our practices sufficiently to keep abreast of our ever more demanding markets and organizations? Can we build overarching processes and measurements that make us much more effective? Can we focus effort and resources only where it makes the most returns? Can we make profoundly better decisions? Can we increase the 'power' of the marketer within organizations, grasp everyone along the way, and show them a promised land of virtuous customer centricity? *YES, WE CAN.*

These 15 compelling and deliberately short bullet-precise mini-manifestos are the initial result from commencing this fruitful and worthwhile journey. Worthwhile for marketers and the organizations and its customers they choose to serve.

The mini-manifestos are the result of a new and innovative marketer-sensing and analytical methodology that 'cuts to the chase' – separating out crucial and potent issues for marketers and market-ing, whilst offering real insight into a basis for breakthrough resolu-tions to those challenges and help to realize opportunities. Each of these consciously practical, individual mini-manifestos examines an underlying conflict, offering some assumptions that underpin and perpetuate that conflict – to prompt and provoke your own interpretations of the problem and help you examine how it relates to your own circumstance and context. **They can provide an exceptional insight into how you may create a particularly strong and sustainable competitive advantage** – and give you a lasting and effective tool to question and improve your own decision-making process.

Reality does not have to be complex

We are conditioned to think that reality is inherently complex, so we constantly look for sophisticated mechanisms to deal with the many differing challenges that face us. The reality of our situation is often not so very complex and the resulting 'solutions' to our continuing day-to-day 'fire-fighting' challenges and unrealized opportunities may actually be more apparent and elegant than one expects. Perceived complexity limits or prohibits the use of the human consciousness and surrogates it to the latest technologies, 'hedging bets' by improving anywhere or adopting that latest three letter acronym and pseudo-science that bedevils our profession! We must resist these pressures.

In reading and examining the relationship between our top priority challenges and opportunities for marketing you will see a developing relationship between the issues raised and the core conflicts articulated in this book; indeed this is no surprise as one may expect important and profound issues to be linked together in a logical way. Common and related causes and effects offer the foundation for a true and vital systemic examination and insight into the profound and elegant changes required within the marketers' domain. These core conflicts manifest themselves as pernicious and unacceptable compromises that prevent us reaching our goals, so we need to break them. The assumptions that sustain them have to be assessed and challenged before any resolution is realized.

The reason that so many of our efforts – any and all marketing efforts, including for example our new product or service development aspirations – are thwarted and fail is that the 'intuitive impetus' behind those efforts ultimately conflict with our view of the reality that confronts and confounds us. That is a major reason as to why we never really achieve the objectives we inherently know as marketers to be right – such as the need to be focused on the customer. The reality that we see infuriatingly conflicts with what we as marketers want to be the new reality. The conflicts explained in this book and their associated assumptions prevent us from resolving this conundrum and making the necessary changes that we desire. However, we *can* address those assumptions, *and* make changes for the better – if we actually see those assumptions before us and attempt to address or negate them in a profound, elegant and pragmatic manner.

This book is fashioned to provoke and encourage you to do this in your own way, so you can clearly see the challenges and opportunities and how things can change for the better when those conflicts are resolved, in your own context. After considering each 'core conflict', we look at WHAT to change, what to change TO and HOW to change to a more desirable situation for marketing prowess and the marketer – which includes an analysis of the underpinning dilemma that has to be overcome, in turn offering a real insight into what actions to take (see Appendices for tips on working with conflicts, and some worksheets for your own assessments).

Whatever course of action you take following your own assessment and interpretation of *The Marketing Manifesto*, I am confident that you will not see the marketing world or your own situation the same way ever again.

A staple maxim of the scientific world is that once you have a fundamental grasp of the problem and it is well articulated, you are almost already at the resolution to it... Now we have identified these issues and have defined them in detail. What we have here is a refined and potent collection of evidential knowledge about the issues that really are of import to the marketer and what in truth stands in the way of virtuous, sustainable and powerful marketing capabilities – both for the company they represent and for each individual marketer.

So just go do it... grasp the path proffered in this Manifesto and liberate yourself from the frenzied conventions of the new and the fossilized chains of the past.

The future of marketing

01

> *Consumers are statistics. Customers are people.*
>
> **STANLEY MARCUS**

Main principle

Marketing is apparently a defined practice and discipline. It is less well understood and defined as a strategic process and the marketer is a long way from being recognized as a high ranking and valued business colleague, when compared to the other C-level top disciplines or professional specialisms such as finance.

The definition of what it means to be a marketer and the operational scope for the marketer and marketing requires to undergo an overdue, radical revolution... **Now.**

Underpinning contradiction and beliefs to confront

The contradiction – the dilemma that prevents us establishing a resolution to the problem – is plainly a question of what *entity* is the priority for the organization: the customer or the organization itself. The realization is that this 'core conflict' underpins our inability to situate marketing where it *should be* in the organization and in the mind of the business manager. This is reflected in the poor status of marketing and the marketer, universally.

Whether one is a marketer, business manager or executive with an interest in marketing, we of course favour a path that follows our intuition which tells us we should be putting the customer first; but we find ourselves putting the organization first instead, at all times. The following illustration (Figure 1) shows us this underpinning conflict, as we try to balance those very different priorities. We have to test our assumptions – why do we have this conflict and why do we find ourselves juggling between the two? The consumer or customer must choose to buy from us, and come to that conclusion through our focus on meeting their needs; yet we have to target custom from those homogeneous market segments that we have traditionally always had to identify and target, based on *our* preferences.

FIGURE 1   Who is given priority?

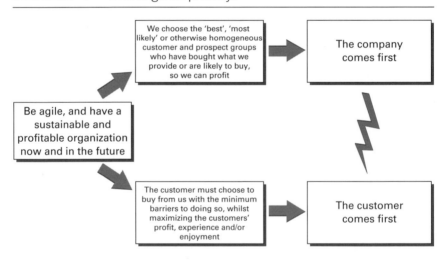

© David J Hood
The Marketing Manifesto™

Testing assumptions

The primary assumptions that underpin the conflict or dilemma illustrated in Figure 1 are listed below.

   1 **We choose the 'best' or 'most likely' or otherwise homogeneous customer and prospect groups who have bought – or are likely to buy – what we provide so we can profit, because:**

a it is easy to identify, segment, and precision-target a suitably large and eager customer base that will pay us appropriately, as we have done in the past;

b growing commoditization and a lack of superior differentiation means we must find them and sell to them quickly, before the dynamics of the market make our products and service propositions and competitive advantage less interesting or obsolete.

2 **Therefore... the company comes first, because:**

a the customer doesn't have priority as we need to 'feed the machine' that is our organization, whilst building our core competencies to produce in the best and most efficient way;

b we have such a well-defined, extremely competitive edge that is imperishable and invulnerable;

c we always have to cut back and focus on doing more, with less, so we cannot 'ride both horses' and thus we have to remain loyal to the organization, even when and where this may conflict with the customer;

d regardless of other considerations, it seems that all the company wants is more sales, month on month, year on year, regardless of the market environment and our ability to compete – so we need to meet the expectations of increasing volume and velocity of sales from top management and shareholders.

3 **The customer must choose to buy from us with the minimum barriers to doing so, whilst maximizing their profit, experience and enjoyment, because:**

a it otherwise becomes proportionately very difficult for the customer to buy (that much is obvious);

b the more hurdles there are to purchasing from us, the more expensive it is for us in terms of lower revenues and higher costs to overcome any hurdles;

c otherwise we make it easier for our competition to win the business from the customer or consumer.

4 Therefore... the customer comes first, because:

  a they pay us, the organization doesn't;

  b they have a choice and we have to match and satisfy their needs otherwise they will go elsewhere;

  c this is the best way to fully support our sales efforts and sales colleagues who, after all, are charged with bringing in the money;

  d competition is fierce and *anything* that may give us an edge – and 'edging the customer towards us' – is worth it.

We need to make a real and profound swing from the current position of marketing fideism to one of marketing fidelity. We have a duty to make marketing a more honest and evidence-led practice.

DAVID JAMES HOOD

Core conflict

It is unlikely that most organizations will truly appreciate the customer and move away sufficiently from simply paying lip service to finally, and *truly put the customer first*. This situation has arisen not because marketers, directors and managers who run organizations do not wish to put the customer at the heart of things, but rather that because of the dilemma articulated above they find it almost impossible to do so. From the above illustration however, we see that the ongoing unresolved *conflict* is the problem. The fact that we are not as good at putting the customer first is therefore a symptom, *not* the problem. Can we consequently find a third way forward? A meaningful and elegant way that is *unmistakably* NOT a compromise (compromising is what we have been doing up until now)? Additionally, can we do it in a way that ensures we realize both necessary conditions that are vital to achieving the main objective stated in the first box in Figure 1? This may all appear a tad obvious. Let's face it, we know that it all starts and ends with the customer or consumer; a number of customers and end consumers throughout the supply chain and in any market. Nevertheless, unless we can finally resolve this conflict, then we cannot say we are true marketers, our marketing will not be anything else but impotent and we will never realize our aspirations for it.

> *The most important adage and the only adage is – the customer comes first, whatever the business, the customer comes first.*
>
> **KERRY STOKES**

WHAT to change

- The definition of marketing, to reflect the reality that is our interdependent world.

- Review and recognize who does marketing, what it should do, and how it should be done.

- The insufficiency of adequate professional and industry standards to apply to the identification, translation and resolution of customers and other stakeholders' needs, challenges and opportunities.

- Nurture and grow the marketer along with the growth of the company (as an exemplar of marketing).

- Marketing as a paradigm, policy and discipline must come of age... *it is high time it grew up and asserted itself!*

What to change TO

- Dump the tired, old functionally based silo and 'putting lipstick on the pig' approach to marketing; change marketing and its practices into a more comprehensive and process-based, strategic corporate management discipline and orientation.

- A realization that every person and every process interacts as a 'marketing process component' that affect as a whole, our ability to deliver and profit (*as human beings we all exchange things – whether it be goods or services, but also cash, information and other items, whether tangible or intangible; these are all exchanges in a 'market' context*).

- Academic standards do exist, but good standard corporate measurements for marketing do not (that would help us break our customer/consumer vs company conflict!).

- Marketers are fully supported and nurtured and must thrive in line with corporate wellbeing.

- Marketing has been a management 'art' for an age, and now it needs to mature into a corporate and robust business science along with its peer disciplines and professions.

HOW to change

- Elevate the marketing process above any and all departments, functions or processes and make it the complete embodiment of meaningful two-way communications and the exchange of *anything* between stakeholders in the business.

- Develop symbiotic marketing processes alongside marketer-development strategies and systems that work in concert. Identify everyone involved in the marketing process and how they can and will be nurtured as 'exchangers of real value added activities'.

- Develop practical, applied standards, for individual marketers AND organizations; to calibrate, maintain and improve their marketing approach, orientation, strategies and so-called 'customer-centricity'.

- Introduce a kite-mark or otherwise recognized endorsement of marketing abilities and orientation.

- Support the marketer with real-time, prioritized, 'focused and leveraged' services, and products based on their evidenced prime needs, the needs of their customer base and those of the marketers' own organization.

- Marketing with, and through the marketer at its centre, becomes THE guiding business science and discipline.

Reflection and action

It is high time that marketing came of age. We intuitively know it is the lifeblood of the organization, that it is worth so much more value to the company and other stakeholders than arguably most organizational activities – yet we need to pull it up by its bootstraps. Let us get rid of 'paying lip service to customer service niceties' and replace this with a resolution to the core conflict.

Take brave steps

- Review marketing, in line with the sentiments given earlier – it is all about the exchange of *anything* – so the marketing process should cover all items exchanged along the supply chain, starting within your own organization.

- Work through the following Manifestos, checking the conflicts offered with your own experiences and assumptions; realize how you could better configure marketing and your own position within the organization to the benefit of all.

- Grasp marketing and inform everyone about it internally. Most people in the organization that are not involved intimately with the customer or consumer (that is just about everybody!) will not know what marketing *is*, never mind what marketing *does*. Educate your colleagues – offer them update marketing training sessions (or something less formal); offer an internal newsletter to give them key intelligence about customer feedback, trends in market needs, and ensure that they all know their usefulness in terms of input as adding value to the overall proposition. Bring the customer or consumer to them all.

- Look for some personal breakthrough answers – *the best feature of using the core conflict/dilemma approach is that it not only allows one to better articulate a problem*, it demonstrates a conflict between two opposing routes, policies or activities. This tends to induce a resolution; an answer tends to jump out from testing assumptions and helps to resolve the conflict and ensure a robust way forward. *Try it – I commend this approach to you.*

"The principle was right there – you couldn't miss it. The more you did for your customers, the more they did for us.

DEBBI FIELDS

What the hell *is* a marketer?

02

> *For a' that and a' that, our toils obscure and a' that...*
> *the pith o' sense and pride o' worth, are higher rank*
> *than a' that.*
>
> **ROBERT BURNS**

Main principle

Marketers are *fortunate* in that they have a really important and worthwhile task – to seek to organize and manage resources to satisfy the needs of the customer, whilst constantly and consistently maintaining and improving our human experience, and making profit for all – however one defines and measures 'profit'.

> *There is never a better place without marketers.*
>
> **A BLOG POST**

Yet, marketers are *unfortunate* in that they don't have much of an unambiguous and decipherable position within the organization and society; they are seen by some colleagues and publicly as something of a hybrid of Alchemist, Snake-oil Salesman and slightly-mad-Creative – with a predictable hint of wizardry.

We are seen, at best, as Tactical Automatons to implement tactics demanded by senior management. This is wholly unsatisfactory and highlights the lack of success to date for our combined efforts to substantially improve the status for the profession and our role in any organization.

This does nothing to help the status of the marketer – or their career – nor does it ensure that the organization takes marketing seriously. Of course, when asked, any director, manager or executive from any organization will state the importance of marketing to the organization. In reality however, the profession and practice is held largely in very little regard, and is less understood by colleagues than arguably most of the other disciplines to be found in any organization. *We are therefore on the 'back foot' from the start.*

Couple this challenge with the fact that in recent years the marketer has had to take on a huge change and revolution in their practice.

With the advent of new technologies and correspondingly greater stresses and strains placed upon the need for a new skill set, the time has never been better, or the imperative greater, to redefine what a marketer is and what they do.

Then we need to go and tell EVERYONE about it. What marketers and marketing does is said to be worth more than three times the value of anyone else in the organization (source: *PA Consulting*) – so it is high time that you were valued, given the reins of those activities and responsibilities that come your way, and better grasp the thorny flower that is marketing.

Underpinning contradiction and beliefs to confront

So what will help us resolve this lack of status and misperception of our role – and how will it liberate our potential to really make the organization thrive?

We have to GET OUT OF THE DEPARTMENTAL CONSTRAINT. We have to include all our colleagues and staff in marketing – and educate them along the way.

We are more than fed up with marketing being seen as a reduced function, a tactical silo for 'telling yelling and selling'™ (*this is a trademarked phrase belonging to the Author's company*) and therefore we need to empower ourselves to help guide the organization, all its employees and management, to greater competitive advantage and superior delivery and positioning within the brain of the customer or consumer.

In order to get out of the 'departmental constraint' we must first check and test some of the assumptions – some held by us, and some held by our colleagues. We must meet them head on – testing them and see how we can overcome those distortions of what we are and what we do – and only then can our fellow colleagues and directors really appreciate what marketing is and what it can do to enable them to dependably improve and sustain the organization. After all, if Marketers can't 'sell themselves' internally to colleagues, then who can?

" *A marketer is a terrible thing to waste.*

BETH COMSTOCK

We owe it to ourselves, those organizations we choose to serve (and our customers and consumers of course), to step up and ensure we are recognized – at all levels, and wherever there is a 'deliverable' that affects the customer or consumer.

The following illustration (Figure 2) outlines the dilemma facing us as a straightforward silo vs pan-company issue – but also offers an insight into a resolution, with a fundamental challenge and change to the notion that marketing is simply a department or function.

This is why marketing is stuck where it is – it is not solely a case of making marketing 'more inclusive' internally, but marketing should move RIGHT OUT of the function or department and embrace all.

Let us change marketing from being a function or department to an inclusive PROCESS led by marketer champions.

A related point is that no one should constantly blame our colleagues in sales for insufficient volumes of consumers, customers, prospects or indeed sales that we marketers or senior management had planned or anticipated. This insufficiency is in large part a **symptom** of the fact that marketing is still not sufficiently 'processized'; if it were, marketing would be 'cooking the market' for sales, and our colleagues there would be left to do what they do best – make and close the deals – and they would sincerely thank us for liberating them to do so.

Local optima (around how we perceive value, the creation and improvements to value and the so-called value chain) also cause conflict for marketers, but we will discuss that issue later in the book.

FIGURE 2   Function or process?

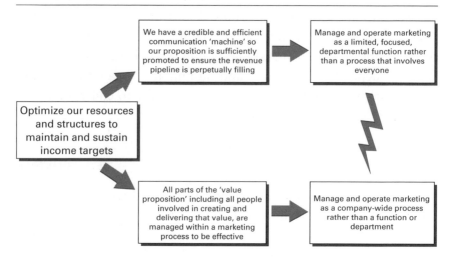

© David J Hood
The Marketing Manifesto™

Testing assumptions

1 We have a credible and efficient communication 'machine' so our proposition is sufficiently promoted to ensure the revenue pipeline is perpetually filling, because:

   a all marketing efforts should be geared towards 'stuffing the pipeline' with sufficient numbers of prospects and customers;

   b we have limited resources to allow for broader issues of improvement of delivery to be assessed and addressed, so we therefore have to concentrate on 'broadcasting' and outgoing communications for current campaigns.

2 Therefore... we manage and operate marketing as a limited, focused, departmental FUNCTION rather than a process that involves everyone because:

a it is pretty much impossible to do otherwise, due to many factors that encourage us to concentrate marketing activities in one place and which reflect the inherent *tactical* rather than *strategic* emphasis for marketing, that is prevalent in most organizations;

b marketing is always so busy securing prospects and weaning them into becoming customers, that consequently there is a feeling that we need to do everything NOW, and we have an urgency to tell what we need to tell to the prospect and customer, as tenaciously and as many times as possible;

c no-one sees marketing as anything other than a means to 'tell, yell, and sell'™, so being seen as an additional creative activity that 'helps the organization sell things at the end of the business process' is about all we can expect;

d inputs and important commercial decision making needs to come from the board, not marketing, as marketing should be the 'reactive storm-troopers' for the business, orchestrated by the board or senior management.

The crucial step of moving marketing outside of the marketing department involves taking people well outside of their comfort zones – marketers outside marketing, and other managers having to learn marketing.

DAVID JAMES HOOD

3 All parts of the 'value proposition' including all people involved in creating and delivering that value, are managed within a marketing process to be effective, because:

a everyone can work in concert under existing or possible structures towards common value determination and delivery;

b a holistic process of this type cuts down on wastage and ensures common goals are achieved;

c it becomes easier to be transparent and to know what each and every individual or function is actually contributing to the proposition and creating profit for all stakeholders.

4 Therefore... we manage and operate marketing as
a company-wide PROCESS rather than a function or
department, because:

a input and decision-making need to come from those who
know where, and how, current and future profits are and
can best be made and fed to others;

b value creation and its delivery cannot be optimized without
a company-wide process; otherwise there is a great chance
that there will be insufficient activity or many unnecessary
improvements elsewhere – or conversely, activity or
improvements that may actually be detrimental to the goal
of the process – and this may jeopardize sales and marketing
efforts;

c otherwise it will not manage or effect sufficient control over
the development or delivery of the 'value proposition'.

Core conflict

A major tension exists between the notion of 'marketing as a process'
and 'marketing as a function' as articulated above, and this manifests
itself in many differing ways within the organization. Take the process
of budgeting for example. Marketing is always seen as inconvenient
EXPENDITURE, a budget line item (and in many organizations often
seen as nothing more than a budgetary afterthought) and is certainly
rarely seen as an investment.

" *The sole meaning of life is to serve humanity.*

LEO TOLSTOY

**Budget setting is an example of a 'management approach by governance
to specification' – a wholly misleading approach.**

Whoever thought that the approach to choosing what would be
spent on marketing – the important process of sensing and responding
to the market – would be judged mainly by an arbitrary question:
'well, what can we afford to spend on marketing after all other
planned expenditure is considered'?

We come across budgets and budget-setting quite a lot in addressing the problems with marketing. Why? The processes of setting budgets for marketing are seen as firm and well founded, rather than what they are – wholly arbitrary with marketing budgeting really seen as grasping (expensive) 'scraps from the crowded table'. This situation is bad enough, but perversely the same mindset forms the basis of many significant management decisions, including the creation of sales and income targets and decisions about new product, service or market developments!

The word 'budget' means 'making financial arrangements, planning expenditure for something' – but what is wrong with using the word *investment*? If we started using the word investment, this would make a huge difference to people's perception of marketing; as long as we could of course begin to better determine and demonstrate with confidence some return on that investment, now and in the future.

WHAT to change

- The status of the 'marketer', as it is ill-defined in the workplace and in business in general.

- Marketers (and many of our customer-facing colleagues) have poor standing in relation to other colleagues in the organization and to business professionals of other disciplines.

- There are no attempts made to define and map out ALL of the marketing roles in an organization – whether those are direct identifiable roles, 'partial' customer-facing roles, or where they may be secondary to their main role within the organization (see mini-Manifesto 9 also on this subject).

- There is a dysfunction where marketer 'role-types' need to be developed and used to help improve and make clear the career path for marketers and their strategic deployment and influence within their organization.

What to change TO

- A new revised and recognized definition as to what a marketer is, and what he or she does for any organization.

- Develop an equal standing between the marketer and other roles and professionals, with similar respectability, authority and accountability, with an emphasis on stakeholder benefit and financial and systemic returns for all.

- A deeper understanding and insight into the use of marketing itself through knowledge of each and every stakeholders' role in the marketing process and involvement in ALL transactions (not only monetary transactions, but physical and intangible exchanges of 'things, data, knowledge and communications').

- Define clearly the marketer's role in orchestrating the development of added value and how they can maintain market sense-and-respond activities and processes that permeate the organization.

HOW to change

- Create a series of new articles and keynote works to redefine a 'marketer' in a modern commercial context that takes cognizance of the current systemic, technological and cultural changes; establish this in the business lexicon.

- Collate and align the academic with the 'practical' components of a marketer's role to make professional standards more robust and easily configurable to help the marketer whatever their role, career path or task in hand to make them better prepared, valued and effective.

- Determine what 'touch point' processes in an organization exist and which correspondingly can and should be influenced and managed by the marketer; how they can do that (and how they will be aided to achieve it); how these points will be monitored, measured and improvements made strictly *only where necessary, alleviating the prime constraints* along the marketing and innovation process.

- **Give marketers the navigation mechanism and an 'engine', along with the corresponding and necessary authority for creating and managing an over-arching sustainable process of ongoing improvement.**

Reflection and action

Humankind is naturally configured for two-way communications; ergo, a two-way marketing 'currency' should come naturally to us. *Companies exist to serve society, not the other way around.* The most important communication is that which is inbound, not outwards. Marketing is not taking cognizance of the human spirit, mind, intelligence or interactive nature and desires that humans have to interact with each other, rather than with machines or sophisticated processes or technologies.

Can we move on from what E F Schumacher described as "the silly or pernicious adult education provided by the mass producers of consumer goods through the medium of advertisements"? One-way marketing is counter to the way humankind is configured, and therefore how our social systems are configured. Functionalism – the way we organize conceptually and consciously and define what we do, by and through structures as articulated in the core conflict – encourages one-way communication, a 'corporate remoteness and aloofness' from the market and inhibits real sensitivity to the needs of our fellow human beings.

A creed for marketing

Our shared mission as a profession must be to help fellow marketers realize fulfilment in the role and context of their choice and to subsequently enable them to lead their chosen organizations and partnerships towards systemic fulfilment for humanity.

A creed for the marketer

Our mission as individual marketers is to enable our organizations to touch and enrich lives in a way wholly unexpected and welcomed and which otherwise may not be realized; giving as great a level of happiness and fulfilment for as many people as possible, constantly and consistently.

Take brave steps

- Put in a new holistic **marketing process** that governs all the marketing mix elements and the exchange of everything within an organization's 'business ecosystem'.

- Educate everyone in the organization and remind them consistently about what marketing is, what it does for them all, how it improves and changes in-line with market dynamics to ensure agility; and how it helps each and every one of them, including paying all our salaries and dividends!

- Review all customer-facing staff inputs and outputs.

- Develop a proper systemic customer-needs sense and respond system that feeds into the marketing process and that evidences any changes to strategy, tactics, product or service development and the competitive process.

Marketing is too important to be left to the marketing department.

DAVID PACKARD

Marketing Futurecast®

03

> *The only thing we know about the future is that it will be different... The best way to predict the future is to create it.*
>
> **PETER DRUCKER**

Main principle

Marketing needs to enable the organization to look into the future. The need to predict is an essential part of good management: to envisage the impact of specific possible issues and events on the organization and seek to orientate the organization, its strategies and plans, to meet those future challenges and opportunities.

Marketing Futurecast® is the new and timely evolution for marketing, making it fit for the 21st century. It is the new means of bringing *robust exploration* to the art of forecasting; conducting predictive scenario planning and using enhanced tools to ensure that we and our organizations are not only prepared to meet future challenges or opportunities, but are able to actually *shape* our own future.

> *Unfortunately, but also unsurprisingly, we try to guide our organization, our marketing, and all of our projections and strategic preparations for tomorrow by continually looking in our reverse mirror. We always look backwards expecting to see a hint of our future. We need to look through the front window at where we are going. The way to do that is through the new prism for marketing, and that is called Marketing Futurecast.*
>
> **PROF LUIZ MOUTINHO**

(The co-author of the latter part of this mini-Manifesto is Professor Luiz Moutinho of the University of Glasgow and the Marketing Futurecast Laboratory at the University of Lisbon and is © copyright. Links to developing Marketing Futurecast® activities, tools and insights can be found on the book's website.)

Underpinning contradiction and beliefs to confront

In addition to the need for a robust and powerful set of tools to help the marketer predict and prepare the organization for the future, there are a number of key hurdles standing in the way. Needless to say, **we would rather reduce the need to react to changing events and market dynamics and increase our state of readiness and be proactive** – and indeed not only be prepared to meet future challenges and opportunities, but to actually *shape* that future as we would wish it to be.

To purport to 'know' future demand is an illusion – at least whilst we continue to use the old hackneyed ways that perform defunct regressive analyses to 'scientificate' our predictions and calculations. We really need to drive forward, based on today and tomorrow, rather than what happened last year!

One of the main hurdles to creating much more powerful predictive modelling or sensing capabilities is the principle that our predicting and reactive response is primarily based on our reliance on **marketing as an agent of the company, not the customer or consumer.**

We pore through the piles of profoundly glib (although statistically compelling) profundity of generic market intelligence and trends; running our scenarios that look deliciously complex (and which usually are, so they usually don't disappoint in that regard at least) from the security of our own comfortable, yet very remote-from-market executive chairs.

It may seem a moot point, and one that mirrors other insights in these mini-Manifestos that reflect on the customer/consumer vs company diadem underpinning many of our troubles (such as that in Manifesto 1) but the inclusion of the word **'agent'** is very important.

An agent acts on behalf of another or others. Surely the best hope we have, is to firmly place marketing – and perhaps marketers – outside of the organization, thereby enhancing their ability to continuously sense the marketplace?

> *In a future where physical and virtual brands' worlds will blend, where any brand will have the capability of becoming a retailer or a medium, no brand will be sacred in its marketplace.*
>
> **PROFESSOR LUIZ MOUTINHO**

As an interesting thought experiment: consider how many business-to-business (B2B) companies you know that would actually place their marketers or company agents, with a responsibility for some marketing aspect, INSIDE the customer's or prospect's domain. (By this, I do not mean people who represent your company installing or otherwise carrying out some kind of contractual deliverable 'onsite', but they are there primarily to sense and feed right into your own organization's customer needs research, development and market intelligence process.)

Who is determining the ongoing and future health and direction for your organization? Is there someone *formally* in charge of strategic change – other than a consideration and discussion about strategy at the occasional board meetings? Who is steering future scenario planning – and on what is it based? Are we, as Professor Moutinho laments, always looking toward our internal regression models for answers, when the real answer, to quote a famous TV series, '*is out there*'?

Are scenario-planning methods, tools and models based on your needs, or are they simply lifted from generic marketing strategies or business case studies, literature or reported practices?

> *No sensible decision can be made any longer without taking into account not only the world as it is, but the world as it will be.*
>
> **ISSAC ASIMOV**

An interesting core conflict that underpins a major tenet of Marketing Futurecast – marketing as an agent for the customer – is articulated in Figure 3. *(Those wishing to examine or enquire about Marketing Futurecast® as a set of tools for the organization are guided towards the book resources in the Appendix.)*

FIGURE 3   The future is out there

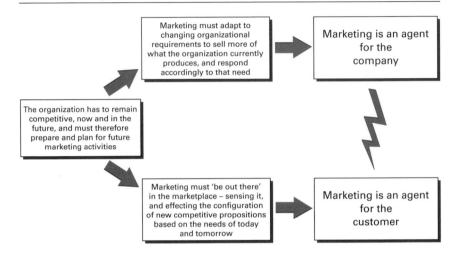

© David J Hood
The Marketing Manifesto™

Testing assumptions

1 Marketing must adapt to changing organizational requirements to sell more of what the organization currently produces, and respond accordingly to *that* need, because:

a scenario planning is inherently and immovably conservative. We simply need to sell more of our current and likely future offerings to the same type of people we have identified and targeted, or are wishing to target, well into the future;

b we have to sell what we have invested in, developed, and subsequently planned to sell and have ready for delivery for the foreseeable future;

c our portfolio of products or services carefully matches our historical capabilities, our core competencies and propositions that fit with each other as a competitive range and sensible 'family' of products or services. This has taken us time and effort to cultivate and must be maintained.

2 Therefore... marketing is an agent for the company, because:

a we need to change and engage our own internal activities – including marketing – to suit the organization's strategic and operational requirements to efficiently make money;

b we have to get a return on our investment (ROI) for *existing* product or services, regardless of what the customer or consumer needs or wants now or in the future;

c we must cut down new opportunities to innovate to those we can handle and are likely to be able to afford to develop and realize at any time.

3 Marketing must 'be out there' in the marketplace – sensing it, and effecting the configuration of new competitive propositions based on the needs of today and tomorrow, because:

a we need to fully grasp and be capable of developing 'what-if' strategies and scenarios;

b someone or something needs to be the constant and consistent eyes and ears of the organization and marketing and the marketer are best placed to provide this role and sense-and-respond activity;

c new products or services or modifications to the proposition lead to new profits and engender renewal of the profit-making capability and opportunity;

d new product and service development resources are limited, therefore we must concentrate on developing propositions that are actually going to make money in the future.

4 *Therefore... marketing is an agent for the customer, because:*

a intuition tells us that product and service development cycles must be shorter (we need it to be; and year on year, it invariably has to be);

b products and services are more likely to succeed if the customer/consumer is empowered in direct terms to 'create' it from their own need (eg what is termed 'Prosumerism', where the customer/consumer has a marked, direct and structured involvement in the product or service being developed and how it may be delivered);

c it is the changing needs of the **customer or consumer** that we need to meet (and therefore those of the marketer);

d no-one else will look after the customer or consumer interest as effectively as marketing.

Core conflict

The issue – the core conflict that stands in the way of good and meaningful prediction and preparation for the future – is related to the first mini-Manifesto, ie *where* marketing is conceptually placed in the collective mind of the organization; and resolution of the core conflict is critical to improving the capability of the organization to effectively 'Futurecast'. As humans, even if we are humans who have managerial or operational decisions and activities to undertake on behalf of the organization, we sometimes take the familiar or easy road rather than look at the difficult and in many cases, more fruitful path.

Traditional methods to predict the future have been largely discredited – and very few predictive calculations and assertions have ever been proven right. The road to prophecy is awash with many anecdotes of business predictions that were shown to be wide off the mark. Or indeed, wholly wrong and extremely costly. What is asserted here is that our usual focus, and locus, is internal; we therefore only 'trust' our own internal data – resulting in our own skewed perspective with which to look at the markets and the world around us. We rely heavily on lengthy regressional analyses; our optimistic and unrealistic 'hockey-stick' type charts, showing new trends that show sales and potential interest in new types or categories of products and services going right off the scale. *We focus on the kind of products and services we think we need to make and markets we think we would like to attack rather than those markets we perhaps would actually want or prefer, or which would benefit us more.* Broadcasted 'industry reports', usually from vested interests and the usual suspect 'business chattering classes' diverts us further from the path to profit.

What we do forget however, is that the prospect, customer or consumer is not driven by those charts or matrices, nor influenced by our analyses and interpretations. **If we think about it sufficiently and look at previous results, we instinctively know that change is happening all too quickly to delve into our past for the results for the key to the future. We need realtime, robust exploratory tools that base their efficacy for sensing and responding on the immediacy of the market, if we ever hope to keep pace with that change.**

We really need to gauge what our fellow man or woman needs, often ahead of the time that the need becomes obvious to anyone. (This is not to be confused with the annoying and damaging 'creating the need before the customer or consumer knows they have it' – an improper presumption that bedevils our profession).

WHAT to change

- The total lack of human sensing, market sensing and common-sense management (CSM).

- The total absence of "brain-to-brain" (Br2Br) in past and contemporary marketing communication.

- Marketing is configured not to be the agent of the organization/ company, but to be a true agent of the customer/consumer and of human beings – the consumer/customer agency.

What to change TO

- From a 'silo' organizational structure into a cross-functional, integrated and process-based marketing management format. Marketers as 'value-added coaches'.

- Old style marketing is outbound by its nature. Inbound marketing would involve listening to the real human being behind the customer or consumer.

- The epitome of customer centricity is not based on discussions peppered with the phrases, 'customer centrism', 'customer retention', 'customer satisfaction' as a preceding adjective... it is SMTG – '... show me the goods'! Moreover, what the current marketers and managers do not fully understand is that, in an era when the customer or consumer has ever more control, these individuals are expecting to participate in the decision making around his or her future.

HOW to change

- The Marketing Futurecast® concept entails the breaking free from the old golden era of marketing, transforming its facets into 'marketing, but not as you know it'. It implies simplificity marketing, commonsense marketing, and 'marketing with meaning'.

- Treat your customers like humans... *do we really need to remind ourselves of this?* Continuously obtain the pulse of the customer and consumer. It is not just about understanding them from the outside, but also getting a real feeling for what it is like to live their lives!... Understanding customers or consumers... with them!

- Brand management is *interface* management. The organization has to manage every link with its customers' personnel, financial, operations, logistics, media, etc to express its brand values. Responsibility for the brand moves beyond the marketing department.

- The customer or consumer, not the brand manager, is the key specifier.

Reflection and action

For once, the possibility is within our grasp – marketers, managers, and organizations can take responsibility for sustainable competitive advantage and corporate wellbeing – and no longer blame ethereal competitive forces or market factors. If you KNOW the customer or consumer better than your competitors, and can SHAPE those markets most profoundly through applying Marketing Futurecast®, then there is no excuse, only a huge opportunity. *Remember – we cannot see what is in store for the organization, its product and service propositions, or for ourselves, if we see things from the inside out.*

Take brave steps

We need to see things from the outside in. As much as the soldier in the trench needs a periscope or some other technology to see the scope of the battlefield and how the battle is progressing, we need advanced mechanisms for keeping track of changes – changes that *matter* – outside in the marketplace; and marketing becoming a true agent of the customer or consumer is part of that process of embedding into the organization the ability to truly sense and shape the future. Get marketing out of the marketing department.

> People ask me to predict the future, when all I want to do is prevent it. Better yet, build it. Predicting the future is much too easy, anyway. You look at the people around you, the street you stand on, and the invisible air you breathe, and predict more of the same. To hell with more. I want better.
>
> **RAY BRADBURY**

Marketing recruitment and resourcing

04

> *Oh, the difference between nearly right and exactly right.*
>
> **H JACKSON BROWN, JR**

Main principle

The entire process of recruitment in marketing is a hit or miss affair. Actually, it is largely a miss – a *mis*alignment between the needs of the organization, the manager with responsibility for recruitment, the existing or new role, the team dynamics, and ultimately the candidate. It fails on so many levels and in so many ways, to serve *anyone*.

Underpinning contradiction and beliefs to confront

Self-esteem is related in large part to your job. Marketers by the nature of how they are employed and the structures, limitations and dynamics of the organization in which they work, have a tough job maintaining and developing their self-esteem and self-worth. It is also really hard for marketers and the professional bodies that support them to improve the recruitment and resourcing processes that are so important to both the marketer in terms of their career path and the immediate and ongoing needs of the employing organization.

Marketing is one of the roles in working life where one is meant to be creative, *yet* reduce any risk. We are meant to be jack-of-all-trades – 'it is just selling to people surely' – and yet masters of them all. We get a lot of responsibility, some could say the greatest in any organization, **getting the money in now and in the future,** yet we rarely have the authority or context required to do the job all the way through from customer need, through strategy, marketing tactics and delivery of products and services.

How can a marketer truly have self-esteem when they are only offered or delegated few of the levers that they really require to meet important commercial imperatives and objectives? Everyone's 'pay-check' is supposedly linked with his or her individual effectiveness – in commercial terms. Our sales colleagues' salaries most certainly are. However, if we are to be judged on what we bring to the company, that is the value developed and realized for the customer or consumer and organization as the result of our efforts, or at least those that would be measured against our role and activities; then surely we need to gain those levers of value control in our organizations?

How does this affect the issue of recruitment? Well, by consistently overlooking a fantastic opportunity to link the remuneration and status of the marketer to be considered for a vacancy, or currently in their role, with new empowering levers that they need, the employing organization is wasting a huge and infrequent chance of making a step-change advance in their competitiveness.

Every recruitment or resourcing situation should be an opportunity for real change. However, every time the employing organization plays safe. It's the same old routine – agency, process, interviews, questions, CV/Résumé, adverts *(that say absolutely NOTHING about the role that someone will have to dedicate most of their waking time to),* 'inductions' and training – **to continue to make them as ineffective and mechanistic as those they are replacing.** Very few recruitment agencies know *anything* about marketing. Just ask around, check with colleagues and other marketers who have recently been recruited through an agency. Ask them how long, laborious and useless the whole experience was. Why is this process not handled by professional *marketers*, rather than 'costly CV shufflers'? I am sure that the employing organization wishes and deserves more – and so does the marketer. *How many vacant roles are filled, or created, that are fully evidenced back to the needs of the organization's customer base?*

Employers have to think further than just filling a seat in the office. Employers have to think further than just securing someone quickly to see through present campaigns. Moreover, what about the candidates, the marketers and managers with responsibility for marketing? They need to see past the superficial adverts promising little and hiding much. They need – nay, expect – a good service that places the candidate where they can fulfil expectations and requirements and can excel in their chosen role. The following illustration (Figure 4) articulates the core challenge behind recruitment and resourcing in marketing.

FIGURE 4   Filling the gap vs realizing an opportunity

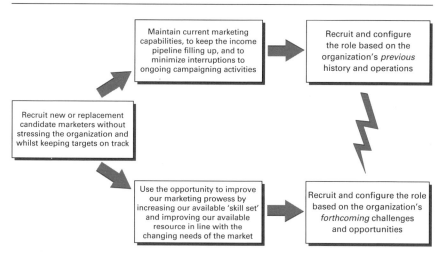

© David J Hood
The Marketing Manifesto™

Testing assumptions

1 Maintain current marketing capabilities, to keep the income pipeline filling up, and to minimize interruptions to ongoing campaigning activities, because:

   a our alignment between strategy, goals, objectives, marketing activities, the team, roles, skills and aptitudes are well understood and has served us sufficiently well in the past;

   b we just have a job to do, and need to be seen to be getting on with it as before, without any break in service to the organization and its current operations.

2 Therefore... we recruit and configure the role based on the organization's previous history and operations, because:

   a we are already as successful as we wish to be, as a profit-making commercial (or not for profit) entity;

   b we see continuity as most important to the organization, its customers, and prospecting activity.

3 Use the opportunity to improve our marketing prowess by increasing our available 'skillset' and improving our available resource, because:

   a we always need to refresh our key skills in marketing, as it is moving so fast;

   b fresh blood should always give us a new perspective to lead us to new competitive differentiation;

   c we never seem to have a sufficiency of skills and aptitudes and always seem to need more to meet ever changing demands.

4 Therefore... recruit and configure the role based on the organization's forthcoming challenges and opportunities, because:

   a it is important to be able to meet the new, developing, and future requirements of our markets;

   b we have immediate needs that are quite different from those in the past when we last took on a new employee or marketer;

   c the customer or consumer also has needs that are quite different from those they had in the past and those needs need to be resolved by an evidential link backwards to new product and service configurations.

Core conflict

The whole process is undertaken as a means to align the suitable candidate with the employer's (very) 'brief' job description instead of aligning the person and role with customer need.

WHAT to change

- The unquestioning loyalty to, and belief in, traditional recruitment processes that are by and large much the same for ALL types of professions or job types.

- The vectors (media and agencies) and the methods used by employers to try to search for and entice candidates to apply for vacant positions.

- The time it takes from promoting the vacancy to drawing up a firm shortlist of candidates.

- The lack of genuine, pertinent, timely and useful information created within the process that would help the employer make better decisions (and also that could help the candidate make better choices as to whom they would wish to submit an enquiry).

- The situation whereby companies have to recruit from a 'standing start', with the barest of information on the candidate (and then find out only *later* if the latter actually fits the role and correspondingly, the role fits the individual too).

- The time, cost and risk associated with such a suboptimal and altogether painful process for all concerned.

What to change TO

- A new recruitment and resourcing paradigm that breaks the mould and is specifically developed for marketing and the marketer, that does not 'commoditize the role'.

- 'Make the jobs real': Do not simply promise more of the same to either the company or the candidates. This is an exceptional opportunity to foster a step-change to profit.

" A man who works with his hands is a labourer; a man who works with his hands and his brain is a craftsman; but a man who works with his hands and his brain and his heart is an artist.

LOUIS NIZER

- The 'funnel' from a pool of candidates needs narrowing and shortening, yet the process of delivery has to be more comprehensive and very deliberate so as to widen and lengthen that funnel – this conflict needs to be resolved.

- Create role definitions based on increasing profit-making and income-generating capability that will harness and interest *only* those who should actually take the job (it shouldn't just be a 'numbers game' relying only on harvesting a sufficient number of candidates).

- Have a 'finger on the pulse' of marketing – or have someone have their finger on it for you – so that finding the best-matched #1 candidate becomes as close to immediate as possible.

HOW to Change

- Totally rip up the usual briefing and poor role description methods along with the entire recruitment process; go and create or find a brand new replacement process and service for the recruitment of marketers and for enhancing marketing resource management.

- Grasp this great new opportunity to create a role that **improves the fortunes for both the company *and* the new recruit.** Mediocrity, and the same-old approach will just not do *(this is a strategically significant recruitment activity and the future of the organization's competitiveness and profit-generating capability can rest on this one decision – not to mention the career and position of the person responsible for the decision to employ the marketer!).*

- Adopt narrow-band targeting of ideal candidates by developing honest, exciting and meaningful roles that augment or replace passive generic human resource recruitment processes and correspondingly terminate the usual practice of poorly promoting unattractive vacancies.

- Align the vacant role as directly as possible with customer-facing objectives and profit motives and subsequent opportunities for improvement to the lives of the customer or consumer.

- You have a process or service that is capable of knowing precisely where to find, who to look for, what role to develop and offer and who to offer it to immediately when a vacancy is created or abruptly imposed on you.

- **'Change the currency' of recruitment** – no longer rely on 'a numbers game', worthless CVs, discredited practices, searching for a candidate whose experience really has no alignment with future objectives or crucial (evidenced!) capability requirements nor with the organization's competitive and customer-centric aspirations.

Reflection and action

In most departments or functions, it is arguably relatively easy to identify what skills are needed for the role or number of tasks, and likewise to identify any shortfall or gap in hard or soft skills. In marketing however, as the world view from the marketer and marketing is pretty much external and the vagaries of the market and changes outside of the organization play strongly on the necessary skillset and other elements of being a marketer, it is somewhat nigh on impossible for the manager, personnel professional or recruitment agent to appreciate the requirements of the marketer – whether that person is a new recruit or an existing colleague.

Take brave steps

- Always see a new or vacant role as an opportunity to improve, not just to continue as before.

- Ensure that the goal, objectives, and all customer alignment issues are included in your aspirations and descriptions of the new or vacant role.

- Ensure that this is all done on a customer-evidenced basis – remember, this is either a developing or new role – **it should NEVER be seen solely as a replacement issue.**

Use a service where MARKETERS drive the recruitment process, in line with your market's current and future needs. Why not? They can add more value to this than anyone else can. That includes most recruitment agencies!

Marketing, finance and accountants unite!

05

> *The cynic knows the price of everything and the value of nothing.* OSCAR WILDE

Main principle

It has always seemed that marketing and its effectiveness as a discrete business activity within the organization, is largely unquantifiable – or at best extremely difficult to measure. The finance and accountancy principles behind organizational accountability and control are however better established or at least accepted; even though the way that corporate measurements, financial management, and their corresponding processes are constructed and utilized should rightly be challenged.

> *Psychologists know that humans are averse to loss more than they are attracted to a gain – perhaps this is a firm explanation as to why cost-cutting and cost-plus attitudes are so insidious in business life. We are basically surrendering everything to playing safe.*
>
> **DAVID JAMES HOOD**

The thesis and reasoning put forward here is that both marketing and finance need to be agitated and aligned; they need to be renewed in parallel to develop combined and evolved measurements and processes to allow the organization (and its market) to survive and thrive.

An interesting point for argument and debate, and hopefully to incite some fresh insight and change, is that the way we retrospectively measure our organization's finances and how we report them hasn't fundamentally changed since the year 1868 (pointed out by Thomas A Stewart, who is a breath of fresh air when it comes to considering and developing the value of intellectual assets and intangibles within an organization).

Balance sheets and P&L accounts have remained much the same for some time, and are of dubious utility as they ever were; and additionally they contain no useful differential between 'good' or 'bad' profits. In addition, people and their vast bulk of the tacit intellectual capital that they contribute – the knowledge that gives us our superior competitive advantage on many an occasion – barely get a mention within any calculations or subsequent corporate accounting reports.

Underpinning contradiction and beliefs to confront

The quote at the start of this mini-Manifesto from Oscar Wilde is prosaic; at least it resonates for those of us involved in marketing, as we occasionally use a version of this quotation, perhaps quite rightly, to tease our colleagues in finance.

I remember, for instance, once asking a room full of top-level finance managers and directors – who will remain nameless of course – what the cost was for this roomful of such an exalted gathering of great brains, and my own modest presence; and whether they could estimate that cost to the *nearest penny*.

They had considered this a challenge perhaps, and all responded with a resounding and firm 'of course' in unison. They had missed an earlier point perhaps – as the meeting was specifically about pricing up their service, based on value, and how we could 'explain' to their customers why they were more expensive than their competitors.

We agreed that in general, **there is a major and apparent detachment and polarization between our ability to track costs in an organization and our inability to value our propositions in the marketplace.** I *knew* that the aforementioned group would probably be able to do that kind of cost calculation, and they probably did it constantly and perhaps even quite consistently, but what they obviously did not manage to do is price their service based on a robust idea of *true* value – the other side of the income/expenditure diadem.

We cannot as marketers be condescending to our finance and accounting colleagues when it comes to making financial calculations and assessments. I am resisting the temptation to do so here, as the **onus is really on us** to get this right; we need to grasp and answer the whole question of Return on Investment for marketing.

Are we ever able to go, cap in hand and a sure-fire ROI calculation print-out under our arm, to the finance director, accountant, board, CEO or fellow managers and make steadfast statements about expenditure and returns for our seemingly nefarious activities as marketers?

Arguably, a marketer's version of Wilde's quotation could read *'we know the cost of our budgeted marketing activities, but not what value it will surely yield'*. Sure, we know where we are going to spend our budgets, but we are generally not so certain about likely returns as are our colleagues who spend their hard-won budgets on other areas of the business.

Psychologists know that humans are averse to loss more than they are attracted to a gain – perhaps this is partly the cause of the rot that is the preponderance for cost-cutting and the indelible corporate attitude that favours 'cost-plus' value determination.

Then again, finance 'counts the beans', and we make sure that the 'beans sell' and continue to do so, to ensure that we get paid and always get paid. The finance people want us to spend less, we want them to increase our budget (and our colleagues in sales also want us to drop the price, which stresses both marketing and finance).

Finance considers their world-view as erring to safe, perhaps more secure than other areas of the business(!) and pretty much full of received wisdom and agreed universal standards; that when thoroughly maintained will ensure the organization stays on some kind of healthy and 'efficient' path to consistent profiteering. Well, we are learning a bit more about corporate measurements and their efficacy these days! However, we marketers and managers involved in marketing are surely less obsessed by efficiency and more by effectiveness? Both are important of course, so it behoves us to find a better way to accommodate both parties, and both views.

Can a new paradigm be found, or consensus reached to place finance and marketing together as two sides of the same 'efficiency/ effectiveness diadem'?

So what is wrong? Surely, we could work on some common framework and measurements, agree common calculations and develop a working and meaningful dashboard that shows both inputs (investments, *not* budgets!) and outputs (bottom line financials and other figures that actually matter)? Oh, and *in real-time*, rather than set months in advance then reviewed or reported on up to a year later, when it is too late to be useful?

There is a conundrum – *a veritable axis of evil* – that is thwarting the best intentions of finance to get the most out of marketing, and the marketer to hit revenue targets and obtain the kind of firm support from their finance colleagues that they would wish. The following illustration (Figure 5) demonstrates this conflict.

Is creation of value for shareholders – something that perhaps exercises the finance director or manager's mind more than most things – **in conflict with the creation of value** as seen through the eyes and mind of the customer or prospect? 'Current' value – the pricing structures and value as the company describes it, in real-time – is easy to calculate perhaps, but future value is less easy, by definition.

The notion or measure of value is somewhat arbitrary and very subjective; would the following people see the same 'value' in an item, service or proposition: the marketer, finance director, operations manager, HR manager, CEO, shareholder, prospect or customer?... *No, they would not!*

> Not everything that can be counted counts and not everything that counts can be counted.

ALBERT EINSTEIN

The CEO's and other top people's salary may be linked with 'shareholder value' (by whatever regime employed, such as EPS – earnings per share, including bonuses and other 'perks'), but how different would the organization's competitiveness and returns be, if their remuneration, along with other senior management was linked to customer value?

Now that is more than simply an interesting 'thought experiment'!

FIGURE 5   The quest for creating, delivering and driving value?

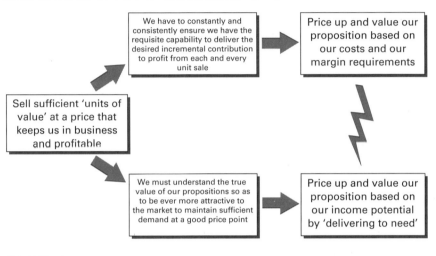

© David J Hood
The Marketing Manifesto™

Testing assumptions

1 We have to constantly and consistently ensure we have the requisite capability to deliver the desired incremental contribution to profit from each and every unit sale, because:

a we need a simple means to construct and operate a management monitoring system that is based on contribution relative to individual units to ensure that we 'sell sufficient units' to cover our costs and make a margin;

b we can adequately align our 'propositions' with our need to make profit by doing things this way;

c a focus on contribution from individual sales helps us leverage our core skills and competencies as we have always done and this has served us well;

    d incremental unit sales aggregate and allow us to consider lifetime-value as a good indicator of consumer or customer worth and allows us to make calculated income targets.

2 *Therefore...* **we price and value our proposition based on our costs and our margin requirements, because:**

    a it is the easiest and simplest way to price up our products and services;

    b we need to ensure significant profit margins and this is a simple and workable way to do this;

    c it is easier to measure, control and manage sales in this way;

    d it allows us to check what propositions are 'making a loss' and those that are 'making a useful contribution';

    e it helps each department 'share' and appreciate their apportioned individual costs and responsibilities; it also allows cross-company comparisons and uses traditional means of operating that most managers readily understand;

    f it helps with portfolio analyses regarding return on investment and apportionment of working capital.

3 **We must understand the true value of our propositions so as to be ever more attractive to the market to maintain sufficient demand at a good price point because:**

    a we actually have a robust and measurable value creation and assessment process already – not just one that simply adds up costs and margins;

    b established price vs demand modelling does not take cognizance of, or help us work towards, suitably differentiated propositions; it may only work for those propositions that are prone to succumb to commoditization. Commoditization and our efforts in productizing deliverables based on OUR values and assertions leads to a conflict with the customer. (See the mini-Manifesto 7: Marketing Misanthropy). It also leads to fighting for a metaphorical share of the 'value cake' with the customer (we want to deliver less, they wish us to deliver more – compromise always prevails);

c there is a downward pricing spiral in many markets; almost all markets seemingly have pricing histories predestined to reductions, but pressures and subsequent actions to get the price-value calculations correct can combat this, prolonging or preventing the onset of those spirals;

d our ongoing and future success is going to be increasingly determined by the market and not our own inventiveness; especially where it comes to value determination and pricing. *(Witness the growth of anti-brand sites and other social networking 'actors' in an organization's environment that can greatly affect the positioning and perception of the organization and its proposition in the mind of the customer or consumer)*;

e we need a grasp of possible future income scenarios and options that will affect our organization's health, income potential and future profitability;

f we know what the customer or consumer needs are and what they truly want, without question;

g it is the best way to build and sustain word-of-mouth promotion and good faith.

4 *Therefore...* **we price up and value our propositions based on our income potential by delivering to need because:**

a any calculation that *we do* to work up a price otherwise is inherently wrong, as we ourselves do not purchase or use the product or service – *they* do;

b there is an unassailable process in place to define customer or consumer needs in place and we use it, and it works;

c we can reduce wastage on ineffective marketing campaigns and on the development or modification of new products and services;

d resolution of need – and the closer we get to it – defines our value to the customer or consumer, our value to the shareholder, and our own personal value as key facilitators in any chain of value-add events;

e our profit as a percentage of revenue must surely increase if we do it this way – we know this intuitively, don't we?

"Any calculations that WE do to work up price points are inherently wrong; as we ourselves do not purchase or use the product or service nor know it's true value – THEY do."

DAVID JAMES HOOD

Core conflict

There is a true and deep correlation between what we observe within the dyadic nature of three major issues:

1 Cost-plus vs value-based pricing.

2 Return on investment (ie predictions vs reality).

3 Budget vs investment.

Looking at those three issues, one should reflect that expenditure in marketing (according to finance and others concerned with aspects of organizational management) is perhaps not as well managed or apportioned with any great assurance; this must be in large part due to the fact that it is considered and handled solely as a 'budget line item' – effectively just a *cost*.

This in turn is reflected in how we treat organizational activities to 'create value' across the organization and how we look at pricing in the market, in that we focus on the cost of everything to the detriment of identifying and developing real value and improved income opportunities.

'**Budgets and costs**'. '**Line items and expenditure**'. *It is pretty obvious that we need to advance and change terminologies and our ethos and ensure we refer to 'investment' and 'value pricing' – otherwise we shall never break from the chains of our poor ROI calculations, expectations and returns. Nor will we change from our path of inadvertent commoditization of our products and services.*

As marketers, we inherently know that commoditization is the nemesis to our efforts at brand building; it leads to greater price pressures and adversely affects brand equity and the perception of our organization and its propositions in the mind of the customer.

WHAT to change

- Measurements: what we gauge, monitor and use as a dashboard to manage our organizations and orchestrate its activities to procure income and profit.

- How we determine value; currently we measure 'value' through add-ons, cross-selling/up-selling (etc!) and increased margins to us – *this is not true or 'added' value.*

- Different departments, functions, or individuals use different sets of data, measurements and ultimately KPIs (key performance indicators) or success factors – very few measurements are *shared* measurements throughout the organization.

- With the greatest respect to our accounting and finance colleagues, who usually provide the 'dashboard' for the company's financials, but (in keeping with the automotive analogy) should finance really be expected to tell us what and where to drive, in what direction, when, and how fast?

What to change TO

- Our financial measurements have changed little since the Industrial Revolution and we have not properly used the power of information and communication technology to better measure our business as a *system*. We measure instead the discrete parts of the business relying wholly on 'yesterday's' data. We need to measure more appropriately to ensure delivery now and in the future, based on the real current and future needs of the customer or consumer.

- 'Value-add' is usually performed as a cost-plus 'make more money for us' activity and rarely in tune with the customer's idea of 'added value'. We badly need a customer-generated, more fully evolved and shared sense of value with the customer and have *systemic* needs driving our perception and creation of true value, instead of consistently poor attempts at nominal competitive differentiation. (The ongoing global financial crisis reflects the lack of a systemic approach to running markets and economies; this is mirrored at the more granular, market sector level... what can we learn and employ from the growing call for a systemic and inclusive approach to the macroeconomics of commerce?)

Unnecessary 'added value' delays the entire new product or service development process and delays time-to-market.

DAVID JAMES HOOD

- We need a common company or 'business ecosystem-wide' set of references to calibrate income and sustainability now and in the future.

- A marketing–finance axis that really helps to drive the business – a true 'double-chambered, heart-like pump' impelling cash investments; let us agree a new, meaningful and comprehensive Dashboard! (A Dashboard that enables the development of superior knowledge for making marketing and related decisions for the improvement of true competitiveness, rather than based solely on cost allocation and historical financials.)

HOW to change

- We can measure thousands of different types of data sets or individual types of variables; but we also need to determine how to reduce them to priority key operational and strategic indicators that link directly between strategy, objectives and the heart of customer need.

- **Dump the cost-plus, margin based approach to pricing,** 'adding value', budgeting and ROI activities and change to a needs-solution measurement process (this should leave your competitors standing still, struck down and marvelling at what has happened and wondering why you are now stealing their customers).

- Strange as it may seem, re-evaluate what profit actually means. Have a systemic company-wide and business ecosystem with a shared set of objectives that ensure all our departments, functions and stakeholders work towards the ***ruthless and total exclusion of 'local optima'***... whilst adopting a true market sensing and responsive system.

Your true value depends entirely on what you are compared with.

BOB WELLS

- Get marketers to work in the finance department, and finance people out with the prospects and customers in the field! Formulate an agreed Dashboard. Give the customer or consumer-facing staff access to the system, its inputs and outputs, with access based on what their needs are in helping deliver to the customer or consumer; encourage the input of their individual and discrete assumptions and perspectives, and of course ***treat those inputs as unique sources of both Intellectual Capital and probable competitive advantage***. If we negate the need to price and value things as single unit calculations by focusing ONLY on the most powerful propositions, we negate the need to measure value based on contribution to profit.

Reflection and action

The core conflict in Figure 5 has another frustrating side effect in addition to the value-pricing dilemma. It actually limits our organizational and cultural *ability* to meet the needs of the customer and consumer. The conflict highlights the fact that although we are fully capable of developing evolved and longstanding abilities to measure just about everything *inside* the organization, we contrastingly do not have the corresponding ability to do much *outside* of it. The conflict also impedes our related capability to identify, calculate, secure, transcribe, translate and manage or build any accumulated knowledge. The development of *Intellectual Capital*, *Intellectual Assets*, and *Intellectual Property* are all adversely affected and seriously compromised by the underlying conflict. (**We use financial reporting systems assuming that we still have Industrial Revolution type *commodities* for sale and this compounds the problem.**)

> *Work towards the ruthless and total exclusion of local optima.*
>
> **DAVID JAMES HOOD**

We also do not fully realize our own staff and employees' intrinsic value to the organization, due in large part to the fact that we see them as adding value as the organization determines it. *Consider this*: people, and their respective talents and worth are left out of financial deliberations for most organizations; we commoditize our own products and services; so we operate sub-optimally both in terms of our potential to grow and build upon our staff's Intellectual Capital AND the Intellectual Property which could be procured by a greater emphasis on value from a market perspective. Thus by definition, we have not properly capitalized on our own potential Intellectual Value AND we are very unlikely to.

It is said (by Thomas A Stewart again) that if an organization manages and cites employees within its financial systems as a means to provide competitive advantage (assuming they provide some Intellectual Capital in addition to 'working'), such an organization has a 20 per cent greater chance of survival. Moreover, it has twice more of a chance of survival if the employees are given shares in the organization – but that is a debate for another day perhaps.

> *By accident, rather than by design, we are failing to break the core conflict and create meaningful value for the customer – resulting ironically in a truly perverse consequence – we inadvertently commoditize the very products and services we would wish to position otherwise!*
>
> **DAVID JAMES HOOD**

Imagine – if you will – what would the further percentage increase be for the prospect of survival and rejuvenation for the organization resulting from looking at value from the customers' perspective? If you increase Human Capital AND Customer Capital, then you increase Intellectual Property and Assets, improve your portfolio of propositions and increase income per employee – if the latter is a worthwhile output to measure of course!

(Note though that customer capital must not be confused with social capital – the positioning and communication competences developed through modern social networks – as that could constitute

more of a media channel and platform rather than true understanding or care.)

I will say it again for emphasis – *we are commoditizing our own propositions, including the organization and its products and services in large part due to the nature of our valuing and pricing policies and procedures.* Perversely, this may be seen as a good thing because our collective behaviour as business people is positively affected by the notion and goal of 'stability', and nothing is more stable in sterile terms than reducing your own product or service to a mere commodity.

By the way – zero waste CANNOT be achieved by just getting costs under control. It can only be achieved by starting at the right place – getting the proposition and the value correct from the customer's perspective.

The unresolved conflict also fosters a 'push' rather than a 'pull' paradigm where we force our product or service into the market, rather than have the market 'pull' it as a result of its preference for our propositions over others. 'Units of sale' actually become more important than what it is that we actually sell. *How perverse.*

The conflict can distort our view of what we actually do as an organization and what we can potentially produce – why else would we have such difficulty in valuing our proposition based on the perceptions of the marketplace? It can also skew and detract us towards seeing new custom as being more acceptable to invest in rather than developing our existing customers. (We harbour a huge presumption that existing customers will buy again anyway to some extent and do not need much of an 'investment'.)

People behave according to how they are measured – therefore if our 'worth' and 'value' as either an organization, a department, a team, or an individual marketer or manager is measured by improper measurements, then we behave accordingly... 'So don't expect any change soon, folks'! We tend to firmly believe and hold dear, our cost+, unit cost, and incremental pricing strategies and policies; because once they are calculated, those figures take on some magical and unassailable virtue of sacrosanctity simply because they can be readily placed into some spreadsheets, and the resulting calculations made with a *feeling* of some degree of confidence.

The evidence is there: too many concepts, products and services are dumped and buried in the graveyard of organization-produced 'added-value propositions' for this to be otherwise. *Calculations relating to the customers' or consumers' needs and wants are altogether harder to place into some spreadsheet.*

Take brave steps

- If we move towards the prospects and customers' perception of value, we can bend or affect entirely the demand-supply curves and related challenges that are primarily associated with increased commoditization.

- Functionality and departmentalism must give way to 'processism'; it is pretty convenient in corporate and organizational terms to have people with similar disciplines and functions collected in some specific department, but **marketing is too lateral with too many touch-points in the organization (and outside of it) to be bound up in one place, limiting its efficacy.**

- Challenge wrong measurements – many of our measurements ARE wrong, review them now – such as:
  - share of market vs actual income required;
  - our value vs their value;
  - new custom vs existing customer;
  - our marketing mix vs the customer's preferred marketing mix *(see the mini-Manifesto 11 Digital Fortress: Permission-based Marketing);*
  - I am also struggling with the concept of income per employee as a means of measurement – supposedly to work out the (added) value of a person in an organization – as I am with attempts to gauge people as Intellectual Capital; this ignores operational capability, tacit knowledge, difficult to code knowledge, what and how they do things, their differing levels of empowerment and status, communication skills – **all fall foul of the pernicious interference and diversion that is the drive for 'local optima'.**

- Realize that creating and categorizing 'budgets' for marketing currently has nothing to do with investment. Introduce policies and processes that flip things the other way around – we should have an objective and more evolved way to determine potential value and income from the market first – then work our way back to securing investments from finance or the board to make it happen.

- Realize that what you sell – to the customer or consumer – is value based on *operating* results, not solely or mainly *purchasing* results. The latter is fine, but should not be the focus. You are, after all, in the business of helping the customer or consumer function better or more happily (as not all buying decisions are made on lowest price or ease of purchase!).

Published studies demonstrate an overwhelming tendency for companies to use cost-driver information to do efficiently what they should not be doing in the first place. To achieve competitive and profitable operations in a customer-driver global economy, companies must give customers what they want, not persuade them to purchase what the company now produces at lower cost.

H THOMAS JOHNSON

- Cease all accounting activities and polices that commoditize our propositions.

- Unfortunately, our focus on the *quantitative* – cost, cost+, then commoditizing our propositions – takes supreme precedence and *obliterates our efforts to improve the qualitative* that would have resulted in better need translation to propositions that then manifest themselves in turn as superior, 'good' profits.

Our age of anxiety is, in great part, the result of trying to do today's job with yesterday's tools and yesterday's concepts.

H JACKSON BROWN, JR

Are we really customer or market centric?

06

> *A satisfied customer is the best business strategy of all.*
>
> **MICHAEL LEBOEUF**

Main principle

'Are we really customer or market centric?' is a good question, as we purportedly seek to strive towards this panaceatic soundbite. If we think our organizations are or would wish to be 'centric', then how do we know how to get there? How do we know if and when we are on the right path to attain it, and will we know when we get there?

Is customer or market centricity merely another buzz term? Is it another faddish phrase borne from the marketer's handbook on obscuration? Are we limited in what we could actually achieve in suitably orienting ourselves around the customer by a number of practicalities – such as the fact that we have to look after ourselves and our own interests, despite the needs of the customer?

Underpinning contradiction and beliefs to confront

As marketers and organizations, we measure scale and depths of markets rather than the scale, depth and improvement of customer or consumer profit, happiness and experience. We measure and aspire to market share rather than seeking to satisfy. We seek to control and corral prospects and customers into some convenient (to us) homogeneous groups so we can prey on and 'shoot at them' more effectively, at a time when we desire to do so.

We may pretend to ourselves and others that this is not the case; we may hide behind the latest faddish technology or buzz words to describe things as being otherwise, *but this is precisely how it is.*

> *Revolve your world around the customer and more customers will revolve around you.*
>
> **HEATHER WILLIAMS**

Otherwise, we would have delighted the vast majority of our customer or consumers and have more business than we would wish; whilst discourse between buyers – professional B2B buyers or consumers – would be talking, buzzing about and blogging good news stories concerning our products and services rather than this being an exception.

Go on – think about the last week or two. What was YOUR experience of some service, or product utility, as either a customer or consumer? I would bet it was not that good, or met your expectations for it. You probably have recently experienced poor service or product delivery yourself, or heard someone else complain about it.

Interestingly, we spend an inordinate and disproportionate amount of our valuable time on studying our competitors' products and services, their strategic and tactical manoeuvrings, and proportionately little on customer need. We cannot see the 'customer-need wood' from the 'competitive forest'. *We are too busy 'keeping up with the competition'.*

Is it really practicable, or indeed *possible*, to orientate your organization – all that it is and does – around your customer or consumer? Is it something that would be truly virtuous, or is it some corporate-speak that is blandly translated into nothing more than a few 'The Customer is King' posters that continue to adorn otherwise sterile office walls? It is difficult indeed, one would think, to have some kind of recognized and accepted panacea – a standard by which an organization could measure and aspire to achieve, that would identify and more importantly enable the organization to be truly customer centric. How would we measure our effectiveness at being truly customer or market centric? We presumably couldn't have some standard definitions nor a means to calibrate our 'centred-ness'. Are we missing the opportunity, simply because this seemingly laudable sentiment and aspiration to orientate towards the customer and market seems too audacious? Figure 6 offers an insight into why this issue remains unresolved.

FIGURE 6   Differing perspectives...

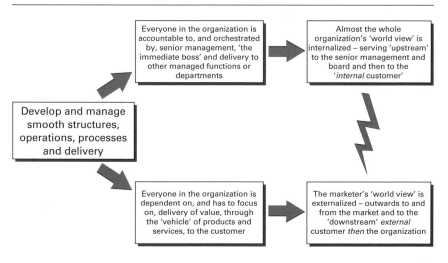

© David J Hood
The Marketing Manifesto™

Testing assumptions

1 Everyone in the organization is accountable to, and orchestrated by, senior management, the 'immediate Boss', and delivery to other managed functions or departments, because:

a there is top-down transcription and translation of strategy, plans and operations and this needs to be managed and maintained in this way;

b the command and control (or what could be called order-and-obey) management method is the only one that 'sees all' and ensures everyone is working in concert and it has always worked this way;

c it would be chaos and anarchy otherwise;

d decisions from the board take priority and are more worthy than other perspectives, issues and possible interruptions.

2 Therefore... almost the whole organization's 'world view' is internalized – serving 'upwards' to the senior management and board and then to the 'internal customer', because:

a many of our staff only see the inside of the company and are influenced and directed by their immediate senior management for almost all of their actions;

b people's behaviour is markedly influenced by how they are measured; so in according them a good management and hierarchical structure, their behaviour can be controlled and coordinated for the good of the organization;

c the management are more important to satisfy than the other functions, departments, and colleagues in the organization (or indeed the marketplace);

d most people in the organization trust others – particularly management – to ensure that overall delivery is maintained appropriately;

e most people only see, especially on a day-to-day basis, no further than 'the door of their department, office, and jurisdiction' and deliver no further.

3 Everyone in the organization is dependent on, and has to focus on, delivery of value, through the 'vehicle' of products and services, to the customer because:

> *Cease calibrating to the beat from the metronome of mediocrity.*
> **DAVID JAMES HOOD**

a without a good and appropriate level of custom, the organization cannot exist;

b the customer is the source of cash and literally pays all the bills, wages and salaries in the organization and remunerates its creditors and investors;

    c wastage is reduced as we only create and deliver what will sell and they in turn will buy, due to a strong and definitive customer or consumer focus;

    d 'non-value-add' activities are reduced and we can focus on competitive advantages that matter and make a real difference.

4 Therefore... the marketer's 'world view' is externalized – outwards to and from the market, to the external, 'downstream' customer, then the organization because:

    a the focus must be on the customer – the market – to have any hope of reaching our aspirational goals and targets for the organization;

    b we can ensure that we only make what is needed and wanted by 'being out there';

    c perspectives of success are different in that delivery of value is the priority: not delivery of hours, things, documents, reports, meetings or some other day-to-day 'beat from the metronome of mediocrity' – that make up everyday noise and associated firefighting.

Core conflict

It could certainly be argued that a significant amount of the pain of our daily firefighting activity (and the considerable time spent on it) is the result of a peculiar interest and unhealthy focus on the internals (the structures, politics, in-fighting etc), that entrance us in the corporate world we inhabit. Had we a greater understanding of our market and correspondingly be able to orientate our organizations in an exceptional but more appropriate way to ensure that we could improve our sense and respond mechanisms, we could and would focus on things that truly matter; consequently spending less of our limited and precious time firefighting and dealing with the detritus that isn't making us any money – and which is habitually causing us to actually *lose* it. In adopting a different 'world view' – an oft used, but very apt phrase here – we not only make ourselves strategically more perceptive of the market, but we give ourselves the means to be a good deal more proactive and responsive. The problem is that it is perhaps only the individual marketer (and the salesperson) that sees the world from the market. *This needs to change.* Simple to declare perhaps, but let us develop a structure as to how an organization could be genuinely customer centric.

> *This may seem simple, but you need to give customers what they want, not what you think they want. And, if you do this, people will keep coming back.*
>
> **JOHN ILHAN**

WHAT to change

- Marketing is something we tend to do TO the customer and not *with* the customer. Why is this the case, when so many of us would want it *otherwise*? (Or profess to!)

- We get PAID for what we do; this is a given in business, as we are all paid by the organization which is in turn paid by the customer, yet we truly serve only the organization.

- Customer or market delivery is seen as being only the domain of front end operations (ie those interfacing with the customer on a daily basis).

- There is no marked, robust and generally accepted description, framework or calibrated and codified means to enable us to configure ourselves and our operations to embrace and maintain customer or market centricity.

What to change TO

- Marketing, as a practice, still requires to match the definition and rhetoric of what it professes to be. (Ironically, the place where it started, in the town or village market, was arguably more true to marketing than what it now appears to be, even with our evolved trading and communication systems.)

- Adopt an outward-inward perspective rather than an inward-outward one. There are many more players and issues outside of our business that will affect whether we survive, thrive or fail.

- Re-examine relationships internally. 'See and show to others' how marketing is a PROCESS that everyone is involved in and resource accordingly. (Currently very few people within organizations realize their own involvement or that of their department or function in marketing and customer value terms; and neither they nor their managers truly know what a vital customer-critical role they may actually perform!

- Establish a good market and customer-centric MODEL, which you can test, calibrate, maintain and improve and which also means something to your market (ie it is not just some type of new 'industry standard').

HOW to change

- Break down marketing into the blend of MODERN MARKETING MIX components (the 17 Ps – *see mini-Manifesto 12 for those mix elements*). How do we fare in all elements of this mix? Do we check to ensure that a) each component is a true, firm two-way street and b) they are all customer generated, evidenced and improved on an ongoing, prioritized basis?

- Adapt all information and communications technologies and other processes or systems to start at the OUTSIDE and work their way inwards. Just think about how often we deal with solely internal data and problems compared to examining and dealing with the external ones.

- Measure and calculate what everyone does and construct a grid for all: two axes a) the marketing mix elements and b) the extent to which this element is affected by the person or department. Map this, benchmark (against the same individual or department over time), and use this as an improvement tool on a sustainable and ongoing basis.

- Write your own particular rules – there is little in the way of market or customer-centric recognized standards (unlike other areas of business and society, strangely), but this WILL change as the need to survive and become more competitive intensifies and business practices evolve.

Reflection and action

Marketing – the people involved in marketing – frequently have less contact with many of the major departments and functions within the organization, as they have what could be said to be 'a foot in both camps' – the market and the organization. They have less influence than many of the other departments and functions, yet they have the most important role and input to ensure that the organization is indeed market or customer centric and competitive.

The organization's world view is inherently internalized, thus assuring marketing's remoteness (both the 'department' and those involved in it) from the rest of the organization; then instead of working towards matching needs with organizational resources for mutual profit, most people in the company and managers in particular end up managing the *side-effects* of not having a market-centric approach – which is constantly having to fight fires.

Take brave steps

- Check your customer acquisition vs customer retention policies – and review them entirely. Do you favour acquisition, and if so, why?

- Whatever happened to post-sale customer service? When was the last time you got a call, letter or some kind of follow-up when you made a purchase? (A great example is the lack of a quick call to your room from a hotel reception desk to check if you are happy with your room and if there may be anything you would wish). Contrast that with our African guide who on vacation, gave us a sterling service and said constantly 'if the Tourist is happy, the Guide is happy. If they are not, the Guide is not.'

- Establish service-related key performance indicators along with the usual KPIs related to products and internal financials and operations. (Coupled of course, with a suitable customer or consumer word of mouth index using a consistent appropriate measurement process to gauge their happiness and experience in being a customer or consumer of your products and services.) You could even nominate or appoint someone specifically for real post-sales service, not just for complaint management!

- Our hierarchies prevent us from ever establishing a customer-centric orientation; try to flatten the structure of the organization to allow for and encourage more contact points with the market and improvement of those points. These new points of contact reflect the reality of the need to network and the unavoidable momentum that is demolishing barriers to real and worthy communications.

- Realize that needs definition can and should now be in real-time. Resource up your front-end customer service to *listen to all feedback*, not just respond to problems. Needs change so quickly that real-time sensing and transcribing needs and translating them must be the new order – *connection with, not collection of, prospects, customers or consumers*. It is not about homogenized segments any more. It is all about connection with the *individual*. We have the technology now, so let's get rid of the excuses and the misleading assumptions standing in the way of exceptional delivery.

- Deal with the conundrum that we are too busy keeping up with the competitor to suitably keep up with the customer or consumer.

- Realize that we have a choice between a corporate policy of wanting customers to bleed vs wanting the customers to grow and have greater satisfaction and fulfilment.

- Any change towards customer or market centricity needs the full-on backing of the CEO... can we have it now, *please*?

> *The vision must be followed by the venture. It is not enough to stare up the steps – we must step up the stairs.*
>
> **VANCE HAVNER**

Marketing misanthropy

07

> Marketing misanthropy:
>
> n (mär'kĭ-tĭng / mĭs-ăn'thrə-pē)
>
> – a dislike of the customer; seeing the customer as an adversary; pessimistic distrust of human nature expressed in individual and corporate thought and behaviour in dealing with prospects, customers, consumers, or partners. **DAVID J HOOD**

Main principle

I read recently of a study that stated that organizations who responded to a survey believed they satisfied the vast majority of their customers. The reality was however quite different, in that their actual customers were surveyed likewise and described the very opposite. Indeed very few of those customers had experienced adequately satisfied needs and wants. The contrast was *startling*.

> Marketing misanthropy leads to an unhealthy sensation of competition and contempt for the customer rather than one of cooperation and common profit.
>
> **DAVID JAMES HOOD**

Why? It is perhaps insufficient to believe that it is just down to a trite or superficial misunderstanding on the part of the company, or more seriously, an inability to listen to and understand the customer. There must be more to this misalignment between the organization's view of itself (and its propositions) and the perspective of the organization in the mind of the prospect, customer, consumer or market.

Underpinning contradiction and beliefs to confront

We are always under pressure to deliver more, with less. Enhance the competitive propositions, but with correspondingly less of a budget to develop, market and deliver them. Less money and resources to support, sense, respond, and perform the ever-increasing amount of activities to perform. This can engender a somewhat unusual and ironic disposition for an organization and its managers – one where the customer is seen as a cost (in time as well as money); a mere irritation, someone or some organization that has to be offered the lowest cost, lowest service possible to keep our diminishing margins sufficiently above zero. The reasoning or at least the underlying reason that doesn't surface to the point that we can readily see it and which is quite similar to the chronic core conflict articulated in mini-Manifesto 5 earlier in the book, is that we are unnaturally *forced into a conflict with our own intuition and aspirations in terms of our delivery parameters to the customer*; thanks to the existence of a conflict that sees the customer or prospect as someone 'on the other side of the balance' from the organization's perspective. We assume, conceive or perceive, that when the customer benefits, we lose. If we win, they lose. Unfortunately, it has been this way for some time, originating from a time when we started to see prospects, customers and con-sumers as *numbers* and *markets* rather than people – and arguably **at that time we actually stopped keeping close sight of them.**

'Those irritating customers. And those irritating prospect enquiries. Those irritating sales agents. They are always on the phone wanting something, and asking stupid questions.' We have all heard it said before, and indeed found ourselves muttering those sentiments (or worse). Anything that gets in the way of activities to hit our short-term targets – which is just about everything anyway – is viewed as an irritation at best; and a focus on delivery, quality, improvements, customer service, and other activities surely would simply detract us from achieving those targets – so we think.

> *We have to reduce the tweaking and redouble the speaking.*
>
> **DAVID JAMES HOOD**

The prospect, customer or consumers' changing needs, their rank refusal to succumb or play along with our tactical ploys and campaigns or sufficiently warming and sufficiently quickly, to our ongoing tweaks to the proposition or marketing mix, all lead to an unhealthy sensation of competition and contempt for the customer or consumer, rather than one of cooperation and common profit. The following core conflict illustrated in Figure 7 underpins and sustains this undesirable situation.

FIGURE 7   The dynamics of misanthropy...

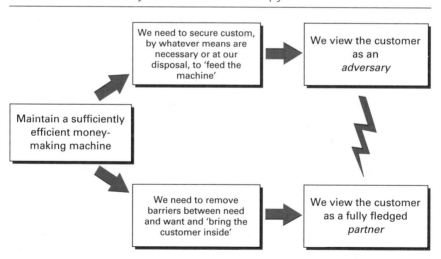

© David J Hood
The Marketing Manifesto™

Testing assumptions

1 We need to secure customers, by whatever means are necessary or at our disposal, to 'feed the machine', because:

a it is all a numbers game in reality and to be in business we need to pile prospects, customers or consumers into that machine, irrespective of the outcome;

b we have to replace churn of old customers dropping out or 'old sales', with new customers and 'new sales', at all times;

c the larger the number of prospects, consumers or customers, discrete markets, and range of products and services we have, the more money we make;

d we have a tall order to meet – to attract sufficient and increasing interest in our propositions at all times – that we have little time to court the prospect or customer and we need to continuously hit them with a sufficiency of messages accordingly or they simply will not buy.

2 Therefore... we view the customer as an adversary, because:

a they have the option to go elsewhere and may not be 'loyal'. We think they need us, when for most of the time they don't even think about us nor care about us;

b we find we have to use a lot of resources (ie money) and persuasion to bring them around to our way of thinking, behaviour, or action required of them by us;

c their own views, prejudices, preferences etc need to be combated so our wishes prevail; they are *fickle*, so we cannot await their *own* need, want or value determination!

d if they hold on to their money, we don't have it in our bank account;

e the more money we spend on delivering the proposition, the less money we can keep for ourselves.

Not being in tune with your customers is like living in an alternate reality; the way you think your customers feel about your product is not always the same as what your customers really think about your product.

BO BENNETT

3 We need to remove barriers between need and want and 'bring the customer inside' because:

a there are too many barriers between us and 'the sale' that reduces any hope of a new or ongoing profitable relationship with the prospect and customer;

b our competitors are aspiring or trying to do likewise and perhaps making a better job of it;

c we can markedly reduce our costs by removing hurdles to the *sale*, rather than reducing the costs to produce;

d it isn't enough for the customer or potential customer to need our propositions, they have to *want* them; so we need to help translate needs to wants, and that means viewing the prospect, consumer or customer quite differently and working closely with them.

4 Therefore... we view the customer as a fully fledged partner because:

a the prospect, customer or consumer requires to demonstrably see we sincerely care about them and their wellbeing. They must experience this sufficiently, so as to remove barriers and we have to offer a genuine level of attention to their needs and wants well above the level offered by our competition and well beyond the prospect, customer or the consumers' expectations;

b we need to see them, and they us, as critical to each other's needs and aspirations;

c today's business world is all about partnerships and meaningful win-win situations, not one-win-one-lose (or both-lose!).

WHAT to change

- Seeing the customer as an adversary.

- The cynical means by which we cajole and coerce.

- Turning our decent prospects into becoming new consumers or customers and yet wholly failing to live up to their expectations once the sale has been made (the former is their objective, the latter is the organization's).

- Seeing 'loyalty' as a one-way process and something we demand of the customer and think we *deserve* by putting misguided effort and thoughtless spin and promotions in the place of real consumer or customer centricity.

- Our lack of respect and trust in our own customers and our failure to treat them as humans: they are not simply numbers to be identified, targeted, or acquired and only of collective importance in terms of share-of-market and overall income targets.

What to change TO

- We are all customers of each other: consumers, B2B (Business to Business) buyers, B2P (Business to Public Sector) buyers, sellers, manufacturers, service providers, shareholders, stakeholders, partners; there is nothing wrong with competitiveness and being a 'good adversary' with the competition, *but not with your customer.*

- Set targets to *over* deliver, especially where it doesn't cost the earth to deliver just that bit more and where you have an evidential insight into your customer that translates into added value as they would recognize, describe and appreciate it.

- Demand loyalty to the customer from yourself and your people – make sure that you *earn* it in return, and do not just expect it simply because you wish it, or because you are providing something to the market, or because you spent a lot of money trying to secure it!

- Introduce a 'brain-to-brain', people-focused approach and delivery and do not rely unduly or wholly on technology or many of the other proxies or surrogates that tend to be inhuman(e)!

HOW to change

- You see the customer as an adversary, as they can readily go elsewhere on a whim; they are finding out information on available products and services by themselves, and you are not influencing them as much anymore, so make it easy for them to find out and connect with you. Most companies work on the very *opposite* premise *(a certain well-known European budget airline I reluctantly use springs to mind)*.

- Don't add bells and whistles to the proposition or over-specify the product or service; check what you *can* do rather than what you *cannot*.

- Put everyone through marketing programmes, with six monthly reviews and refresher day courses and workshops. Get as many internal people to 'meet, see and hear' the prospect or customer as opposed to read about them in a newsletter, report or printout!

- Re-humanize all processes where it makes a marked improvement to the organization's revenue, operating expense and inventory (see mini-Manifesto 10).

- Measure efficacy of your word-of-mouth management method such as that outlined in my book 'Competitive SME', and use it wisely – not just to validate your assumptions or possible tactics, but to ensure that you can build and maintain a flourishing relationship with your market and a healthy brand position within it.

Core conflict

The best characteristic about this issue is also its worst. It all revolves around the core conflict that is our perception of the customer. This should make it easy – on the face of it – to change our perceptions of the customer in the grand scheme of things, but it really is surprisingly difficult to see the customer as anything other than an annoyance, a 'necessary evil'. *Oh, if it weren't for those damn demanding customers...*

Reflection and action

Stop seeing the customer as a non-participatory blob of inertia. See them as willing, participatory intelligent human beings with a marked interest in ensuring that *their* world – whether it is a domestic consumer or a professional customer buyer – is altogether safer, happier, running smoothly and they are getting the most out of life. They are participatory, but only when they see you as being likewise. Oh, and *wholly and recognizably sincere.*

Marketing, as a refreshingly new business agenda and active discipline in the past few decades, promised to herald a new era where customers and consumers were back to simply being *people*. An era where the emphasis was supposed to move from the organization to the people and other organizations that pay money to it. That utopia has been prevented and replaced by a dystopia where marketing is encouraged and seen to actually work against the interests of the buyer, and marketing misanthropy is one peculiar and unwanted related effect of marketing's dysfunction.

Take brave steps

We can move our 'cost focus' from reducing costs of delivery to one of reducing cost of sales and income generation through improved and meaningful new ROI policies and measurements and using them accordingly. *Radically* shake down your marketing mix to the *salient mix elements that actually matter* – and make the decision and commitment now that it is simply not right to feed the corporate machine regardless of the consequences and correspondingly annoy the prospect, customer or consumer in the process. Do not seek to short-change your customer or consumer and see them as an adversary. *That does not make any sense at all.*

> *Indifference and neglect often do more damage than outright dislike.*
>
> **JK ROWLING**

The problem with marketing... is the repugnant word!

08

> *Language habits of our communities predispose certain choices of interpretation.* **EDWARD SAPIR**

Main principle

I must offer a disclaimer that I have no real problem with the word 'marketing'. I do not wish to offend any of my fellow marketers, but many of our problems exist because of this seemingly innocuous little word. Everyone has a different understanding of what marketing is and how it is performed, and this causes confusion within the profession and with our colleagues in other disciplines and departments.

Additionally, we marketers are probably quite fond of our profession and business subject; and we know from where the word derives. However, it is the general *use* of the word, especially as a verb in addition to a noun; its associated jargon, our faddish predilection to new terminology and 'gobbledygook', that is causing misinterpretation, misunderstanding and misuse – and all of this has accumulated to prevent acceptance of marketing as a clear and bona fide business discipline and practice. Is the general way we use the word and term 'marketing' and how we position and promote the practice actually serving it, and us, well enough?

Underpinning contradiction and beliefs to confront

Whatever description or definition you use or have heard used, it invariably begins with a reference to 'customer need'. Laudable, and we should expect a reference to the customer and their needs, right there, right at the start, of any definition for marketing. **The difficulty is where the description goes from there, from a noun to a verb,** (thereafter we do not really move far from first base), and how poorly marketing is viewed by others, and surprisingly, how we marketers seem to view and portray it *ourselves*.

Some time ago, I half-jokingly put to an audience of fellow professional marketers that we could really shake things up for the profession, giving it a new impetus and putting it back on track, if we simply removed the words 'marketing' and 'sales' from the business vocabulary and created a brand new business term that encompassed both disciplines, wrapped up in a new definitive description. This was rather warmly welcomed, and perhaps – no definitely – was an unexpected response. It was also suggested that this could just simply be the term 'business development and strategy' but this did not feel sufficient. Why did I table this notion? Well, we were discussing one of the primary difficulties facing the marketer and our profession. *Misunderstanding.* It is easier to describe other disciplines or professions, perhaps, as ours is the least well understood – not only by our colleagues in other roles, but also indeed by *ourselves*. Our 'Institutes' and other membership bodies and learned organizations that feed into (and off!) our profession do not address this important issue at all.

In seeking to 'sex up' what we do, we focus on the received wisdom, case and academic study and frenzied buzz attributed to very high volume FMCG and 'big corporate brand spend on creative works'; we could thus all be forgiven for feeding off the populist sentiment that marketing in its modern context is seen to be **nothing more than 'colouring in the brochures and putting some polish on** what the organization produces' or 'putting lipstick on the pig'. Using alchemy to make the unworthy worthy. We really need to do a job on the word 'marketing'. Irony abounds again – the very profession that should be able to put one word to pole position in the mind of the businessperson, with appropriate and firm perceptional positioning, is marketing. An irony not lost on many of our fellow marketers, and one that along with the fact that they are about the poorest served profession by their own professional membership bodies, completes this veritable humiliation! How can we expect to acquire the status for ourselves and the profession to which each and every one of us aspires? We have only ourselves to blame if we, the people tasked with ensuring a suitable profile for thoughts, ideas, perceptions and brands in markets, cannot revitalize and reposition our important profession higher up the corporate and commercial food chain. The following illustration (Figure 8) articulates the underpinning core conflict.

FIGURE 8   We like the term 'marketing', but it is misunderstood

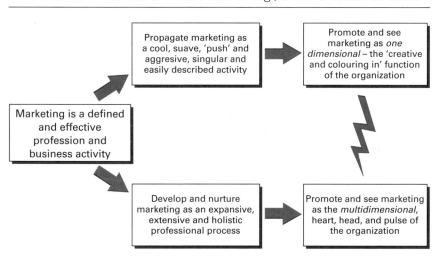

© David J Hood
The Marketing Manifesto™

Testing assumptions

1 We need to propagate marketing as a cool, suave, 'push' and aggressive, singular and thus easily defined activity, because:

  a the 'profession' and its professional support and membership organizations have propagated and constantly reaffirm that this is what is expected of us as individuals and practitioners;

  b it is easier to define and develop marketing if it is seen as a narrow, and sometime lesser, activity;

  c we are seen to be cool, creative types and we can often dwell on it; we aspire to develop that creativity and demonstrate how cool we are and what it is that we do;

  d it is difficult to describe what we actually DO for the organization otherwise;

  e due to the lack of robustness in our discipline, we use 'smoke and mirrors' to hide the fact that we don't know how to best configure our marketing activities for the *greatest return*, so we make up all those new fangled words and phrases... such as 'share of mind' rather than hard-and-fast income objectives. This perpetuates the creative and snazzy image of marketers; although this feels OK, as we can constantly and intentionally add new befuddling words and phrases to the business lexicon and reinforce these perceptions;

  f we are at all times having to convince others of our plans and actions, to listen to us properly and to help secure a decent marketing budget from the corporate 'pot of cash'; *so perhaps to be seen as one-dimensional at least may get us some budget!*

2 *Therefore...* we promote and see marketing as one dimensional – the 'creative and colouring in' function of the organization, because:

  a we cannot blame anyone else – everyone thinks that is just precisely what we are, and what we do is merely applying some spin or sizzle to our produce – and of course some less flattering descriptions are also used!;

b it sounds like we are focused when we do things 'to' the prospect, customer, consumer or market; it makes us sound more convincing and in control... at least we think it may sound more convincing to management, peer colleagues etc, but it doesn't chime with either the customer or consumer (who do not want to be communicated 'to' by marketing!) nor the world at large *(ask anyone not in marketing what it is and does – go on, pick up the phone and speak with a colleague or trusted associate now!);*

c colleagues – especially those in senior management and at the head of the organization – like to hear of us simply projecting messages into the market as it makes them feel as if they are directing us effectively; and when senior colleagues hear about the company from others, those colleagues correspondingly feel more important as more people know or recall who the company is and what they provide;

d it is easier perhaps to ask for a budget for tactical activities that are more easily explained, simply constructed, easily corralled within our own department or function and close to our chests; we need to be clear about what we do in the organization.

3 **We develop and nurture marketing as an expansive, extensive, and holistic professional process because:**

a giving marketing a wider remit will lead to greater effectiveness than simply keeping it within the bounds of 'cleverly creative and pushy campaigns';

b we need to be able to conduct necessary changes to the proposition (the fuller modern marketing mix described elsewhere in this book) and have the *evidential authority* to do it;

c **no-one else** will look after the interests of the prospect and customer nor be able to 'sew up and leverage the loose strands of a business and its necessary revenue generating propositions' towards the profit or other goal;

d generally, the quest to understand all the sub-types and different areas of marketing is otherwise less of a priority for the business (marketing is seen as being outside of the other business functions and quite disconnected, strangely. This has to change.).

Where misunderstanding serves others as an advantage, one is helpless to make oneself understood.

LIONEL TRILLING

4 Therefore... promote and see marketing as the multi-dimensional heart, head, and pulse of the organization because:

a we need to 'move it (marketing) from out of the marketing department or from the individual person or team of people' and encompass all marketing activities other than just narrow campaigning;

b we, and the important role we provide, the activities that we preside over, implement and colleagues we influence, will otherwise never realize their full potential;

c otherwise, marketing will always be seen as a 'single response resource' dedicated to spin and 'colouring in' rather than the 'helm that guides the organizational ship' towards constant and consistent profits through developing and delivering a very comprehensive competitive advantage.

Core conflict

We truly and genuinely – both as individuals and as organizations – wish to streamline and focus our activities. Unfortunately, in doing so, as is demonstrated by the core conflict, we significantly narrow the scope for marketing, for ourselves as marketers, and the ability of the organization to better deliver to the customer.

WHAT to change

- Marketing as a term is the right one, but is sorely misunderstood and references to it misrepresent what is carried out in its name – something we marketing practitioners actually propagate!

- Marketing is seen to be little more than advertising, with some promotions and sales thrown in.

- It is confined within the one word, and as such appears to be separate and dislocated from 'business', or 'strategy', 'sales' and the other business facets that are or should be *wholly and substantially integrated with marketing*. Arguably, marketing should actually be leading and informing those other facets of the business; if only the organization adopted the correct interpretation of the word and embraced the appropriate status and orientation for marketing within its structures and processes.

- Marketing is therefore inextricably tied to the premise and perception that it is a malevolent (and sometimes malignant?) creative art rather than a comprehensive and virtuous business science – it is just seen and practised as a means to coerce and get people and organizations to buy things they neither really need nor want.

What to change TO

- Adopt a refreshed and firm perspective and received status for what marketing actually is, what it does, and what it is really capable of (remember, it is said to drive three times more value for the organization than any other 'function').

- Reinforce marketing as a distinctive (yet boundary-less) set of processes that includes other processes commonly misinterpreted and considered as being the reserve of some other business discipline or department.

- Build the marketing process upon all the other elements of business and have them all **pivot and subordinate this to the customer and other stakeholder needs.**

- It was – and is – a virtuous professional discipline, practice, philosophy and process. *It is time for marketing to take its central, strategic role in the operation of any organization.*

HOW to change

- Reinvigorate the word and general understanding of the word 'marketing' – take an audit of what processes, functions and people interact with the customer, and include **any and all objects, data, money, tangibles and intangibles, that are exchanged** both within and outside of the company. Adopt a holistic, horizontal, process-based approach. *(The exchange of 'things' between structural components of an organization is far more important to the sustainable health of an organization than the corporate structures themselves; yet marketing is seen solely as a function of those structures and is subordinated to them, other than for some of the more apparent exchanges.)*

- Devise marketing-led and customer-centric methods and tools to 'carve out and indelibly maintain' marketing throughout all functions, people and processes involved in your 'business ecosystem'.

- Gear the organization for the 'primacy of the market' and ensure that all staff (and your market) understand what marketing is and its importance to the individual, organization, customer, the health of the company and the longevity of its competitiveness.

- Get all major Professional Membership Organizations (PMOs) and interested groups and parties together to leverage marketing as the 'prime pulse of performance'* for business. (Tough task, but SOMEONE has got to do it!)

  * *The term 'Prime Pulse of Performance' is copyright.*

To know what you prefer instead of humbly saying Amen to what the world tells you you ought to prefer, is to have kept your soul alive.

ROBERT LOUIS STEVENSON

Reflection and action

We need to take stock. Are we sufficiently brave to break out of our conceptual shackles, to stand up and be counted as the multi-skilled and multi-dimensioned professionals we are, dealing decisively with the fact that we are 'jack of all trades and masters of none'? Or are we content to be seen as being tacticians in a narrower field, hemmed in but easily identifiable as people that simply turn out a good story for the organization and propel it sufficiently into the marketplace?

I am not so sure that there is an easy answer. We do need to inform almost everyone in business about the breadth of talent one needs to be a great marketer and what we bring to the organization. We need to win over hearts and minds of our colleagues and management. But then again, is the task too great?

> *When I came into marketing, I found that many of my new peers were suffering from what was unmistakably a kind of marketing mimosis: they were each copying the other's misrepresentation of marketing.*
>
> **DAVID JAMES HOOD**

Are we satisfied to remain practitioners within some clearly segregated sub-element of marketing – providing one or a few of the mix elements or tactical communication channels for instance – or do we ensure that we command access to knowledge that helps us to focus in on the parts of the mix and our strategic requirements in which we require to specialize? Therein lies the subtle, but powerful, difference. Can we provide leadership or are we content with being seen as followers... albeit master-tacticians, rather than seen and appreciated as fundamental strategists and navigators?

Take brave steps

Perhaps, at least for now, we should take every opportunity to tell and yell – that's what we are supposedly good at after all – to whatever appropriate audience we can, precisely what marketing truly brings to and fosters for the organization. A reassessment of how to deal with the long-term problem of misunderstanding about 'that word' and how we address the imbalance between perceptions and potential, is perhaps still some way off. Oh, and then we should probably turn our efforts on addressing those other 'profanities'... the repugnant word and phrase 'consumer' and selling 'solutions'... but maybe that is for another day... or another book...

> *The structure of a language affects the perceptions of reality of its speakers and thus influences their thought patterns and worldviews.*
>
> **THE 'SAPIR-WHORF' HYPOTHESIS**

The marketing and sales standards

09

The quality of a leader is reflected in the standards they set for themselves. **RAY KROC**

Main principle

It took a long time, but now at last we marketers have some underpinning practical standards – thanks to the Marketing and Sales Standards Setting Body (MSSSB) in the United Kingdom.

These Standards are well worth examining as a basis for a functioning training and personnel needs assessment tool in addition to ensuring the organization (and the individual marketer) has a solid foundation for developing a framework to gauge and nurture the organization's pool of marketing talent.

Never before in the history of business and commerce has the dynamics of trade necessitated such a need for constant re-evaluation and updating of core skills in every part of the organization – none less so than in marketing. By and large, we have to contend with new accepted practices, new paradigms, new methods, new tools, new philosophies and new challenges and opportunities; and all of these seeming to change daily.

Until recently, we have only had recognized Academic qualifications to attempt to fill the gap and ensure some kind of standards exist – but nothing readily offers guidance and a practical means to inject professionalism into the practice and grow and improve the skills of the marketer in their existing role and throughout their chosen career path.

Thanks to the MSSSB, we now have a core list of skills that allow us to map and steer our individual and collective marketing capabilities in a way that reflects a more pragmatic approach and helps with the actual *practice* of marketing out there in the 'big bad, cold, world'.

Underpinning contradiction and beliefs to confront

Our profession has been dogged by a lack of standards. (Unlike other professions, there is still no need for a marketer to have ANY formal qualifications or proven skills in their trade.) We have had to rely on straightforward academic study and resulting qualifications to offer some small degree of robustness, progression and direction for the profession. Academic input into the marketing world has not met the burning need for sustainable and realistic operational and workable personal and continuing development frameworks to help ensure that individual marketers or marketing resources meet the strategic requirements of the organizations they serve, or the changing market dynamics in which they actually practise.

We have had a need for good practical and progressive standards for some time. We still have some challenges to face and a host of good opportunities to capitalize on; *so we should be encouraging not only ourselves but also our organizations and the wider business community to embrace these new standards as tools that if used appropriately, can help to fortify and future-proof competitive advantage and engender sheer marketing excellence.*

The number of individual skills necessary to be a marketer and the huge number of individual tactical abilities we are expected to exhibit means that we need to do two things urgently. The *first* is to create and apply standards that are sufficiently wide ranging to enable all elements of marketing to be covered by a set of related and linked standards, and *second*, we need to realize that no two marketers or no two roles are alike in both a strategic and tactical context. So we have to ensure that these, or any other standards need to be focused and 'cut down' to the crucial, critical skills (soft as well as hard skills and of course complimentary behavioural attributes are important too) that are necessary for the marketer to strategically and tactically carry out their responsibilities.

The underlying core conflict is articulated below in Figure 9, which suggests that it is high time indeed that we have a practical set of standards and that these could and should be **directly linked to our agility** – both as individual professional marketers and as organizations.

FIGURE 9   It's time for some real practical standards

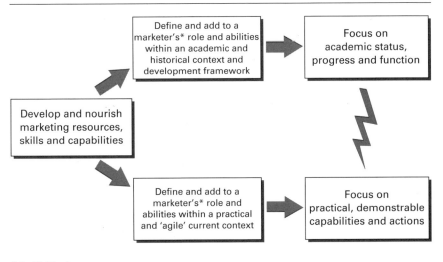

© David J Hood
The Marketing Manifesto[TM]

Testing assumptions

1 We define and add to a marketer's* role and abilities, within an academic and historical context and development framework, because:

 a we understand in academic terms what we have as a marketing resource, and maintain it in those terms (as we do with all the other professional roles within the organization, so why be different here);

b academic qualification should give a marketer sufficient and suitable grounding in the practice to which they are committed;

c academic qualifications are the way that marketing abilities have been defined and are still defined, by the profession itself and have been for many years now (in attempting to define roles and professionalize the discipline);

d academic standards are sufficient to enable the marketer to effectively carry out all their strategic, tactical and campaigning activities, now and in the future.

(* or *any* of those we choose to include within a marketing process or function)

2 Therefore... we focus on academic status, progress and function, because:

a as individuals, we wish to be seen to grasp the academic, arguably wider implications and understanding of whatever profession in which one seeks employment or specialization; and a business qualification is accordingly understood to be useful in the career development of any professional;

b the marketer needs to be developed in line with Human Resources and CPD (continuing professional development) policies that include academic study and achievement, and the department's or functions expectation's for the *existing role and requirements of the position*;

c it helps put us 'on a par' with our fellow professionals within the organization and in business generally;

d the academic-led development of our individual abilities and our profession is adequately supported and improved by those custodians who maintain and deliver those academic standards.

3 Define and add to a marketer's (* as above) role and abilities within a practical and 'agile' current context because:

a we need to be able to conduct the necessary changes to strategies, campaigns and tactics that involve new skills and capabilities at almost every turn;

b an understanding of all elements of marketing knowledge is less of a priority than the ability to deliver the required salient and important immediate actions to meet the specific current and pending challenges and opportunities that face the organization, which change at any particular time.

4 *Therefore...* we focus on the practical, demonstrable capabilities and actions, because:

a real-world marketing is more about the effect of our ability to execute activities, inputs and outputs, strategies and campaigns coupled with the ability to work appropriately with and fully orchestrate our colleagues towards shared objectives; and it is less about demonstrating knowledge about the application of marketing *elsewhere* (at a different time, context, organization or otherwise 'not the case here');

b marketers and others involved in marketing are judged by their ability to bring in the money, not by what they know about marketing – but they do need to know about the new, timely, innovative marketing techniques over and above the old traditional elements to marketing taught by academia;

c we have the specific and necessary *immediate* individual skills already identified that match the organization's goals, its objectives, and customer and market needs and we have mapped them out carefully to hone our agility as an organization.

The standards will help build a new image of marketing as a socially responsible discipline.

DR CHAHID FOURALI, FOUNDER, MSSSB

Core conflict

One could almost describe the conflict as being between 'just in case' marketing capabilities and know-how with 'just in time' marketing capabilities and know-how.

As with many professions or roles, an individual is informed of many differing options he or she has in their role to strategize, plan and act; and quite a lot of that information is presumed to be knowledge. It inherently is, but unless it is useful and applicable, and more importantly it is timely and offers a priority over other issues or information, *then it is not much use at all*. 'Just in case' information is not knowledge – although I am not putting forward the case here for eliminating Academic study or qualification – it just does not cover the latest available information (which is primarily what a marketer has to deal with). Nor does a glut of general information offer a means of honing the skills of a marketer to better meet the specifics of their own *current* role, context, or competitive position and marketplace dynamics in which their organization actually operates.

> *Common sense is instinct. Enough of it is genius.*
>
> **GEORGE BERNARD SHAW**

We do have to be careful though when we structure a robust framework at an organizational, corporate and professional level using any new standards; vigilant that we do not fall foul of glib sentiments that lead us into using the standards inappropriately and then *simply find ourselves standardizing capabilities and skill sets* across organizations or functions.

We could actually find ourselves with an opposite situation than the virtuous one described earlier – where instead of ensuring we honed our abilities to that which were needed at any one time, we created a veritable plethora of 'standard job categories' or other such 'expected level of skills' required of a marketer or someone in a marketing role, at various levels and with various responsibilities.

Therein lies a real danger though, and one I foresaw when I was consulted in the creation of the standards. We could be constructing yet another beast that unnecessarily and unwittingly obfuscates – creating a comfortable smokescreen and diversion that takes us *away* from what is needed by the individual marketer and the company at any particular time and *replaces and usurps it* with what is 'expected of a marketer in a certain role or level within an organization'. Standards replaced by *standardization*.

What we need to do therefore is align the standards with a proper, recognized needs definition process that links ALL the way back from the organization to the market. *To the customer or consumer.*

If we ever hope to work within and build truly customer-centric organizations, then marketing, customer-facing, and customer-value-building skill-sets employed within the organization have to *uniquely* match the requirements and dynamics of the specific developing market context and the place of the organization within it. Development of the marketer needs to be customer centric too!

We can only do this if we know WHAT the needs of the market are of course... otherwise we will continue to train and fortify ourselves with 'just in case' information and skills, rather than 'just in time', 'real' and powerful immediate knowledge and corresponding agility...

WHAT to change

- The less than robust means by which customer-facing individuals, roles, and marketing capabilities are focused around academic qualification and indeterminate and poorly defined descriptions of desired or required skills.

- Useless organizational personnel or continuous professional development appraisal schemes that ignore the appropriate, timely and specific development of the marketer and all the people involved in the marketing process who are key to strategic and operational success.

- The lack of involvement from all involved on the board and top-level management in understanding their place within marketing – they ALL have a marketing role to play and all need to be an integral part of the marketing sense and respond process.

What to change TO

- The Marketing and Sales Standards Setting Body (MSSSB) in the United Kingdom is determined that the standards become a valid currency for the maintenance, improvement, uptake and successful deployment of marketing skills rather than just relying on academic 'worth' of the individual.

- Identify necessary strategic and tactical skills that can be measured, to have the appropriate blend of skills and attributes to deliver strategic and functional capability through the individual marketer and customer-facing people now and in the future.

- Develop the ability to determine what standards would best map key people and roles within the organization and make all in the organization aware of marketing, what it does and identify how the organization will need to develop and nurture elements of the standards for each person, in each role, whilst keeping all within an overall process *rather than isolating each role in the organization as discrete functions, which then suffer from local optima.*

HOW to change

- Develop more 'usable' delivery and promotional mechanisms for the standards to be successfully absorbed and to help marketers and their organizations use the standards more powerfully, specifically and appropriately; effectively we need to better 'productize' the standards into recognized frameworks for delivery and development at different organizational levels, to allow and accelerate their uptake and use in a precise, surgical fashion.

- Translate the needs of the customer or consumer, for the near future (up to three years) into marketing and sales standards sub-sets that precisely map out the skills gap in your marketing capabilities, people, team and company to align and meet those needs; set up a system with Human Resources to monitor and upgrade this at any time (also consider linking this with any Intellectual Asset Register – it will create some wonderful intellectual assets over time).

- Tie in any formal performance appraisal processes with all of the staff and board's understanding of the customers' or consumers' issues and marketing skills development: the staff and board will all have different customer knowledge, level of involvement and corresponding skill requirements – from simple 'awareness' training programmes or induction sessions to fully fledged specific marketing roles. This appraisal process must include all the board members and senior management in the same way that appraisals are applied to other areas of the business.

Reflection and action

Make yourself aware of the standards, examine them carefully and clearly with your Human Resources people. Take care to see how best to use them, and don't fall into the trap of using them as a *prescriptive* set of skills and characteristics 'that all good marketers should have'.

> *Marketing and sales skills are instrumental in helping increase the value of products and services and enable British businesses to better equip themselves in this day of fierce global competition.*
>
> **SIR DIGBY JONES**

The standards need to be carefully used in a coherent way to ensure they become a sharp tool for the marketer and the organization and not used as something that will only act as a disappointing surrogate for examining and sensing what skill sets are needed that actually match the product and service requirements from the market.

Take brave steps

- The appropriate use of the Marketing and Sales Standards is important when mapping out the involvement of ALL of those in the organization who are concerned with and have a customer-facing role, or a defined (by you) added value activity. *(See The Marketing Manifesto* ™ *and Global Marketing Network online resources in the Appendix for access to information on the standards.)*

- Remember different contexts exist – different from organization to organization, marketer to marketer.

- The functions included would cover, but are of course not limited to, marketing, sales, consumer/customer services, product-service development, R&D, shipping, production, delivery, operations, accounts and even such supporting areas as reception staff.

- Work with those responsible for Human Resources or personnel to identify those customer-facing colleagues and develop a plan as to how to engage with them, inform them about marketing, and how to identify and develop the distinctive role in the marketing process that they have to play; and vitally, set up a process to ensure all colleagues work in tandem in-line with strategic marketing objectives and activities.

- We need to use these standards (or others) carefully and focus on the specific skills necessary to deliver the strategic Marketing Mix of today and tomorrow, not some 'pre-formed promotional prison' of yesterday.

- Define your requirement for definitive standards:

  - To ensure marketers within the organization can do the current and future tasks required of the job effectively *(academic standards do not by themselves assure that the marketer is able to perform the role required of them and meet the expectations of the organization and the marketer's own aspirations for the organization and themselves).*

  - To balance and inject **reality** into what is seen as an ethereal art, to all in the organization.

  - To calibrate capabilities, potential and gaps for the marketing *process* (first) and the marketer or other staff member (second), before generalist academic or other 'nice to have' training and development initiatives.

Not every difficult and dangerous thing is suitable for training, but only that which is conducive to success in achieving the object of our effort.

EPICTETUS

Re-humanization: humanity strikes back!

10

> *Communication technology keeps getting in the way of communication.* KYLE EASTHAM

Main principle

Whilst we drive ourselves towards greater personal and organizational effectiveness and efficiency, we tend to lose the personal touch. In an age when differentiation is so dependent on the personal touch, and consumers or customers' trust in companies is at an all-time low, is it not now high time we considered re-humanizing our operations?

Underpinning contradiction and beliefs to confront

Ever since the dawn of the Industrial Revolution, we have hastened and oriented organizational development effort towards simplifying and smoothing business tasks and how each task relates to others within the entire organization. We have successfully introduced robotic manufacturing systems, applied new information and communications technology, cut costs down to a minimum, removed certain key hurdles in our business and production processes, reduced waste and leveraged our scarce resources and skills to good effect.

However, when did we start to think that, when calling our company on the telephone, a customer would be held forever in some digital 'Press 1 for this, # for that' nightmare, and that so many other supposedly virtuous technology-based 'enabling' devices and replacements for human engagement, time and effort might actually have a detrimental and opposite effect from that we had anticipated? I think that if we were honest with ourselves we would consider that many so-called innovations, technologies and 'non-human interventions' are **nothing more than a surrogate for true human-to-human contact.** Let us face it, it was and is, rarely about effectiveness and more about efficiencies. Figure 10 explains:

FIGURE 10   Is it a question of what we are delivering and deploying?

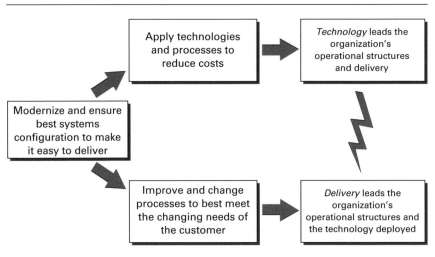

© David J Hood
The Marketing Manifesto™

Testing assumptions

1 Apply technologies and processes to reduce costs, because:

a reducing costs is compatible and congruent with good delivery of our propositions (products and services) and making it easier to deliver;

b most of the technologies that we have or may consider to facilitate 'improvement' to our organization and its operational effectiveness has or will ultimately reduce our costs or otherwise they would never have been considered;

c otherwise it is not reducing costs, but adding to them;

d we need technology that lowers our operational costs to be more competitive.

2 **Therefore... technology leads the organization's operational structure and delivery, because:**

   a technology should and must replace people wherever it can, eliminating fallibility, fragility, fatigability and introducing efficiencies and reproducibility;

   b we place our faith in technology as that is where proficiency and most modern competitive advantage now lies;

   c we are responding to internal needs, and the needs of the board, to hone down our costs (or more likely try to take a mighty scythe to them) and assign or in some way engineer out unnecessary or repetitive tasks through the use of new technologies wherever we can;

   d we completely understand where technology can be used, how it should be used and where it should not;

   e we have a handle on what effect any new technology will have both *indirectly and* directly for our business (including the effect on income throughput rather than just an understanding of direct costs);

   f we need to squeeze costs from all elements of operations and delivery to keep competitive.

3 **Improve and change processes to best meet the changing needs of the customer because:**

   a it makes commercial sense to do so, I'm told, to meet their needs; and this is what we aspire to do as good marketers and managers;

   b it maintains longevity and agility;

    c *their needs and processes are constantly changing and we need to make sure that our processes and delivery mechanisms fit with those used and preferred by the marketplace and continue to change to fit the next requirement or challenge in the market.*

Marketing is being taught and practised without even a basic understanding of human nature, other than what it wishes to accord to it: indulgent and maximized consumption for the singular benefit of the organization.

DAVID JAMES HOOD

4 Therefore... delivery leads the organization's operational structures and the technology deployed, because:

    a our income and profit are ultimately earned and 'pulled from, and by, the market';

    b our ability to deliver excellent propositions effectively is the obvious starting point to orientate resources and calibrate any other ongoing improvements;

    c we know specifically what the market wants in terms of the complete end-to-end, enquiry-to-delivery process and beyond, and how or if, the customer or prospect *evidentially* would wish any of that process to be automated or delivered through some deployed technology (and we strive to give them an opportunity to input into those decisions);

    d technology and processes should always pull human beings together – as that is what we humans are predisposed to do, *to serve each other* – and any new technology deployed must smooth the path and enable both parties to do better trade, and not act as a hurdle in any way.

Technology is the knack of so arranging the world that we do not experience it.

MAX FRISCH

Core conflict

We have an obvious dislocation between what we would like the technology to do for us and what the customer or consumer would like to be in place to actually help *them*. We configure technology based on what we want – witness the meteoric rise of CRM (Customer Relationship Management) and the contradiction that the consumer or customer really does not wish to have a relationship and neither do they wish to be *managed*. All the form filling and input (and output) side of the CRM equation was for our own benefit, not theirs, and this continues to be the case. It was all about selling more, selling more often and 'oh, by the way, we can put a field in it for our contact's birthday' type of so-called customization. *Big deal.*

> *Aren't you tired of having to talk to machines and sit waiting in queues that may not even really exist, while horrible music repeats itself over and over for eternity?*

JESSE S SOMER

WHAT to change

- The ridiculous subservience to technologies, for the sake of keeping up with external and internal expectations.

- Putting our current and new processes and technologies before people (including the consumer, customer, supplier and our own staff).

- Remove and replace our unhealthy, unbalanced and unbridled fetish for cost-cutting.

- Treating people as a commodity, to be replaced continuously as a 'resource of last resort' when the technology cannot be found or fails to deliver.

- People buy from people – so make it so – and make it easier for them to do so.

- The deteriorating and disingenuous throttling of any *person-to-person axis* in selling and delivery to the consumer or customer through inappropriate emphasis on *person-to-technology* axis (and to little else).

What to change TO

- Technology is the slave, the facilitator; it should never be viewed as some kind of unbridled agent for progress; it should be placed only where a human touch is less effective – let us put technology in its place! It should only be considered **when it is removing a major and primary constraint within the business or in the marketplace** – and only where a resulting 'solution' or intervention has been *evidentially* shown a requirement for technology rather than a human being.

- Cease the strategy of replacing people with processes and seeing new processes, configurations of operations etc consequently to be an excuse to cynically reduce head-count.

- We surely have cut costs all we can – **presumably we have become adept at this a *long* time ago** and had *too much* practise at it – and instead *place technology where it maintains, or better still, makes more income for the organization by making its people more effective.*

- Treat people truly as befitting that which is supposed to be your best asset; make them the default resource of choice; don't subordinate them to cost-cutting alternatives.

- Re-humanize your front (customer facing) and back (supplier facing) and outward (all your 'publics') operations and the information gathering/intelligence mechanisms and plethora of communications systems.

- *Go and take on a customer role for two weeks! Try out your own technology and processes sitting alongside them and see just how 'human' they really are!*

HOW to change

- Create a decision-making process that helps make technology and other process improvement introductions that are introduced *only* where such alternatives significantly and completely address precisely identified *core* conflicts.

- See an opportunity for change to be an occasion to **free up more people to *serve*** – whether to serve internally or externally – and take more of that time to have them listen and be inspired by you, develop innovative ideas, or they could give some *free* time to the customer (investment like this is far more rewarding than reducing head count!).

- Cost-cutting is destructive; make a change NOW and ring-fence five times more time and people than you currently do on your cost-cutting deliberations to profit and value improvement and *cut costs only where they are an evidential and virtuous part of a core conflict resolution.*

- Treat people as 'assets of first resort' again; think 'how can I free up their time to give free stuff to the customer.'

- Make your organization a lot more accessible – invite contact between the organization and the customer through blogging and using social media networks at various levels for example – and create a 'virtuous virtual systemic marketing system'. If you cannot 'own it' do not worry as the customer may own it anyway, so keep in with them. Better still, re-evaluate your use of focus groups and use the opportunity afforded by the technology to really revitalize your two-way communications through more appropriate use.

- If you are a manager or executive with a customer-facing role, spend time with the customer; for a day or a week, and do this as often as possible, at least quarterly.

Reflection and action

We can and should be a deal more sensitive – both to the needs of the market and our own people – as it makes very good business sense to be a little bit more discerning about the selection and application of de-humanizing technologies and processes than we have been in the recent past. Actually, we should be a *lot* more discerning. Business and commerce is all about humans helping fellow humans, supported by the technologies and processes that we have created to serve us. It is not about some humans, or groups of humans, capitalizing on using their one-sided technologies and processes to reduce human interaction and in doing so inadvertently or consciously *sterilizing* global and societally based market systems. The human approach to marketing is more than mere 'interaction ergonomics' of how the organization wants the prospect, customer or consumer to interact with it, and much more than a question of 'function', 'usability' or 'accessibility'.

Marketing – and any improvement – must be based on a volte-face approach to interaction, recognizing that the basic human character has been lost to business ever since the Industrial Revolution put the company and the customer or consumer at more than an arm's length across a cart or a stall at a market. *Incidentally, if you wish to see real marketing in action, a good lesson is to check out the local farmers' market – an exemplar and vital reminder of how it used to be and where marketing started.* (This issue – Re-humanization – is closely linked to the issues identified in the following Manifesto 11, Digital Fortress: Permission-based Marketing.)

Take brave steps

- Introduce a new *prioritization* and decision-making process; to decide where and how technology should be introduced, and importantly, where it should not be.

- Use technology as a last resort, rather than people.

- Don't just follow trends to purchase new technology because:

  - your suppliers, who are selling you some technologies and new processes, think you should have it just because everyone else has it;

  - trends are set by the chattering classes and some very smart promotions – less so unfortunately, by consumers or customers;

- – you will have to field hard questions when you don't have the best technology – but it is a lot harder to field questions as to why your consumers or customers have gone...

- Resource up rather than down and increase your human-to-human interface experience and 'touch points'.

It has become appallingly obvious that our technology has exceeded our humanity.

ALBERT EINSTEIN

Digital fortress: permission-based marketing

11

> *Your own mind is a sacred enclosure into which nothing harmful can enter except by your permission.* **ARNOLD BENNETT**

Main principle

Why all the digitized, 'digitally re-mastered' diatribe of confusion for the customer and consumer? Why does 'new' mean new problems, channels, apps, gizmos and platforms, new things we have to develop and do, and in turn new things that the consumer, customer or prospect has to *learn to do* – rather than creating truly new and *appreciated* value and better delivery of that value? Moreover, why 'digitally assault' at every opportunity?

We could all benefit from taking a look at a *systems* approach to marketing – where technology and new digital communications reflect a common development and technical integration roadmap, and one where permission for engagement with the prospect, customer or consumer market can be given or refused, easily. A plethora of electronic devices and delivery methods does not really give us options... it just correspondingly gives us, and our market, more issues to deal with.

Technology in the digitized world is enabling the marketer and the organization to consider wider and more varied options, and so are the advancing marketing vectors and channels. However, the prospect, customer and consumer are slowly but surely gaining control over all those channels, helped in turn by increasingly proactive lobbyists, the developing new legislative influences and strong peer connections between the prospect, consumer and customer.

Remember, permission marketing is applicable to more than just e-mail. More than just the new digital platforms and channels or merely an issue for direct mailing.

Underpinning contradiction and beliefs to confront

In the new era where the customer, consumer or prospect can make more informed and appropriate choices, part of that decision-making and choice process is to choose whether they let you in to their world.

> *The mass market has split into ever-multiplying, ever-changing sets of micro-markets that demand a continually expanding range of options.*
>
> **ALVIN TOFFLER**

Legally, morally and now increasingly commercially, it makes good business sense to ensure that you do indeed have the recipient's (as that is how we view them!) specific permission to contact them and *disrupt their lives* to try to engage with them; selling our products and services as forcefully, efficiently and as often as we can. Asking permission for us to legally assault them carte blanche with 'what we wish to do to them' messages is not permission-based marketing, it is *permissive* marketing. We assume, lazily, that we have that right to do with them what we will – all because the recipient has ticked some box or otherwise supposedly or inadvertently sold their soul to us. The ethos supporting the notion that we have consent to do 'what we wish to do to them' is ignoring the essence and point of permission-based marketing and this diverts and detracts; making us adopt a position that is accordingly wholly inadequate, inappropriate and very dangerous. Why is it dangerous? Because it leads us into a false sense of security that we have some kind of special relationship with the recipient/prospect/customer/consumer, when we obviously have no such thing. Quite a few contenders exist for the underpinning causative conflict in permission-based marketing, including:

- budgets vs Return on Investment (covered elsewhere);
- the need for sufficient probity of information (by the individual customer, prospect, or consumer to make more informed lifestyle, purchasing, utilization of products and services etc) vs the need for 'voluntary simplicity' (ie keep the amount and complexity or nature of information crystallized down to what really matters, is of marked appeal and relevance, and has to be timely; all of which is a good description of what they most certainly want from us);
- push policies (promotion into a void – selling what we make) vs pull policies (being asked by an informed customer or prospect about what we can do for them, right now);
- our power vs customer power;
- organizational power (our organization's) vs legal/political power (the latter emanates from those entities that regulate the commercial world) regarding our respective ability to send and receive messages;
- narrow our focus and reduce communications to those that will be acceptable and accepted vs widening communications to make sure that we get our messages to the prospect, consumer or customer sufficiently often;
- the consumer, customer or prospect themselves wish to narrow the messages that infest and disrupt their lives, yet they also wish to widen the net of opportunities to buy things that are more appropriate and more appropriately priced (the latter phrase does not mean cheaper!);
- another is the overarching moral, thorny and contentious issue of privacy!

We have to choose how we will conduct ourselves more appropriately as digital, technological mayhem gives way to consolidation of devices and channels, or future 'one to all' boundaries or firewalls applied by the receiver. The more advanced mechanisms employed by the prospect, consumer and customer to thwart our communication attempts will be able to close down digital communications within a number of platforms and devices in a single stroke. Permission-based marketing is therefore not just about the question of obtaining the right to interfere or disrupt using some communication or other. It means a defined set of rules that the organization must adhere to so that the market, consumer, customer, prospect and other influencers and 'Actors' in the competitive market abide by certain checks and balances; those measures will encourage greater specificity, timeliness, considerate and altogether more fruitful encounters leading to better alignment of need and resolution or satisfaction. We can – and do – ignore the real dangers and potency of permission marketing at our peril. We have to make some tough, but necessary, decisions *now*. Figure 11 offers a core conflict starting point to address this issue.

FIGURE 11   A digital fortress, and an empowered prospect, customer and consumer

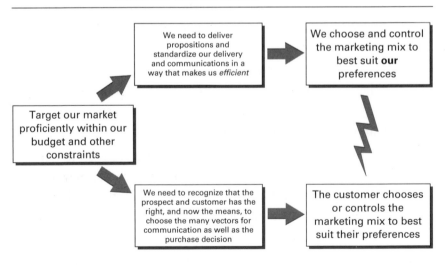

We need to deliver propositions and standardize our delivery and communications in a way that makes us *efficient*

We choose and control the marketing mix to best suit **our** preferences

Target our market proficiently within our budget and other constraints

We need to recognize that the prospect and customer has the right, and now the means, to choose the many vectors for communication as well as the purchase decision

The customer chooses or controls the marketing mix to best suit their preferences

© David J Hood
The Marketing Manifesto™

Testing assumptions

1 We need to deliver propositions and standardize our delivery and communications in a way that makes us efficient, because:

   a as we all easily 'sing to the same hymn-sheet', marketers try to grasp any opportunity to address the consumer, customer or prospect and those groups must wish and want to know what we do, how we do it, and will always expect us to make contact and will welcome our advances with open arms;

   b we constantly have to find new ways to target the market with our messages and make the best of our budgets, therefore we are stuck with constantly reducing the cost per contact with the customer or prospect (and the overall cost per sale and lifetime cost for developing and maintaining contact);

   c it costs us a lot of money to deliver messages routinely to our targets and many messages may not be received; so more messaging, more often, must of course be better to ensure our markets will hear us.

2 Therefore... we choose and control the marketing mix to best suit OUR preferences, because:

   a we can cope with and manage our budget better when we can plan our preferred marketing mix to suit our board and management, our own operational skills and entrenched 'operational habits';

   b we have to overload our customer, consumer and prospect 'just to make sure something sticks' *(This is the jelly on the wall effect – most falls off, but if one throws enough, some will stick)*;

   c we are sufficiently powerful in the marketplace to be able to control the proposition and all elements of the marketing mix and plan them well in advance, and are 100 per cent confident in that marketing mix.

3 We need to recognize that the prospect and customer has the right, and now the means, to choose the many vectors for communication as well as the purchase decision because:

   a otherwise our communications will be immediately or eventually blocked by new overt and stealth prospect-controlled technology, legislation-backed societal and privacy policies and laws, and sheer customer or consumer want or ability to do so; *(or indeed may simply be brought on by inevitable 'promotional fatigue' – you may be excited about your propositions and current or planned changes to the marketing mix, but they will most certainly be less so)*;

   b it makes sense to focus on where they are at in terms of their preferred contact requirements and what THEY wish to do with US (if indeed they do);

   c it is profoundly stupid for us to deny this reality exists and is increasing in magnitude and concern.

4 Therefore... the customer or consumer chooses or controls the marketing mix to best suit THEIR preferences, because:

   a prospects, customers and consumers are time-starved, ill disposed to annoyance, and are ever-more aware of their power and indeed their own needs and options to better satisfy them;

   b technology and legislation is firmly enabling opt-out or preventing opt-in by proxy;

   c we avidly and wholeheartedly embrace this change; actively get them to choose their own mix preferences.

Core conflict

The driving force behind communication and delivery through the new and evolving digital channels is the desire for efficiencies, *far over and above that for effectiveness*. It is self-evident that we are constantly looking to save money, to increase our many 'touchpoints' and then maximize the chance of some interaction with the prospect, consumer or customer; but we are not necessarily seeking to actually *improve* that contact or interaction with them if we are to be brutally honest with ourselves.

Insipid interruption rather than intelligent interaction is no longer acceptable in engaging with your prospect, consumer or customer.

DAVID JAMES HOOD

We could be forgiven for our sins in this; the area of high technology and digital marketing has really not been with us that long and it is galloping along faster than we can comfortably keep up with it. We continually feel like we can do little other than try the latest tactical throw of the digital dice and gamble that we don't upset too many prospective or actual consumers or customers.

As marketers, we know intuitively that fragmentary tactical gambling with the latest technology is simply not good enough.

WHAT to change

- The lack of any clear, recognized, and universally applied legal, technical and industry collaborative standards for integration of all digital marketing channels, products, services and technologies to facilitate ease of use, co-development and co-creation of products or indeed any common set of useful and appropriate codes of practice for permission-based and particularly digital marketing.

- Create a technical and operational convergence of different platforms and channels to help them communicate and avoid or reduce conflict between them.

- Consolidate and reduce the constant, consistent and frustrating need to push and coerce the market into having to constantly learn new habits. *Platforms, technologies and processes should adapt to human need and behaviour, not the other way around.*

- Grasp the opportunity to orientate your digital platforms, channels and feedback systems around the prospect, customer and consumer rather than just trying to interrupt these people 'as often as possible within budget.'

> *Permission marketing is the privilege (not the right) of delivering anticipated, personal and relevant messages to people who actually want to get them.*
>
> **SETH GODIN**

What to change TO

- An integrated means of digital marketing delivery – ie mobile/TV/internet/electronic devices – all platforms increasingly integrating, but with a strong sense of purpose to uphold privacy laws and ethical standards.

- Parallel this renewal with a firm grasp of the trend that is moving toward 'customer–consumer pull' rather than simply pushing new digitized messages to them through new platforms and in all manner of ways.

- Let the customer or consumer choose and wholly compose their own 'digital marketing mix of channels, platforms of preference and contact points.'

- Focus on the means to grasp the opportunity that permission-based marketing affords the supplier and the customer or consumer.

> *Permission marketing envisions marketers and consumers as partners in creating a marketing mix... co-creation.*
>
> **DEB BAKER**

HOW to change

- Commoditize and standardize the languages, code, and technological communication between devices (perhaps there is or will be an effective and appropriate open-source pan-platform technology available for us all to use).

- At the simple side of technology, it appears at the time of going to print that (reluctantly, I am sure) the manufacturers of mobile phone and such small devices will have common and similar battery charging devices – dispensing of the need for an individual user to have a bank of chargers for different types and makes. This (if indeed it happens) is a worthwhile and welcome first step perhaps towards common sense consolidation to singular standards. *Much more needs to follow in all areas of business technology.*

- **Overall, this has the virtue of forcing the supplier/supply chain to consider delivery of value rather than obsess and focus wholly wrongly on the method of delivery.**

- The customer and consumer will hide behind a DIGITAL FORTRESS of our own creation – because we have not engaged with them appropriately; we have just asked them to conform to our preferred contact point technologies and platforms and frankly annoyed the hell out of them!

Reflection and action

This issue of 'their marketing mix versus our preferred marketing mix' could be said to be one of a **focus on effectiveness versus a focus on efficiency**. In spending our money wisely – our hard-earned budgets and hard-won share of company expenditure that we manage to secure and spend on marketing – we see return on investment as simply spending our allocated money in the way that we think makes us efficient. Or at least as efficient as we have been to date with previous marketing activities. We measure enquiry per dollar, euro or pound. The more eyeballs poked, ears that have bled, brows beaten forcefully, arms fully twisted or enquiries per unit cost, the better we think it seems for us, especially when it comes to looking at the outputs of our campaigning; explaining them, accounting for them, and participating in marketing meetings and the annual staff/HR 'corporate dance' aka company appraisals.

However we are putting our trust in simply spending money based on how WE wish the market to interact with US and on the face of it this may save us money in some way; but what can be guaranteed is that we are more likely to be **losing REVENUE** on the other hand by not following what the market wishes us to do in terms of THEIR marketing mix preference.

It really is a question of their measurements versus ours!

We need to better use those digital platforms and vehicles to let the market pre-select us from the mass and morass of competition out there. We need to adapt marketing research and sensing our prospect, consumer and customer by providing more immediate realtime input that helps us achieve permissions appropriately and where it is distinctly an advantage to the prospect, customer or consumer. Will market research in its classical guise be replaced by consumer/customer/prospect search? Social network punditry seems to speak with one voice in support of this prognosis.

Certainly, with the advent of social networks and peer-to-peer recommendations ('share and compare networks') and overall development of the internet and the associated technology that allows prospects, customers or consumers to interact outwith the direct sphere of influence of the organization we are now bearing witness to a major societal and commercial revolution. We are a long way however from these networks being used appropriately by organizations; witness the problems where brands stumble into this world haphazardly – indeed I even hear the phrase 'we need to *own* the conversation with and between the customers in those social and business networks' time and time again. *Organizations, and their illustrious representatives in marketing, should know better.* To try and control communications – as we have aspired to and sometimes 'achieved' in the past – simply alienates the individual or buyer and leads to the opposite of what you as a marketer would wish to achieve. At least with online search and now social networks (for fast-moving consumer goods – FMCG – business to business – B2B – and business to the public sector – B2P) there appears to be a major step in the right direction; but it is in the hands of the marketer and their organization whether they grasp this opportunity to listen intently, to question the very core of their customer-sensing apparatus and policies and to ensure that they don't see search and social as simply another broadcasting or narrowcasting channel to berate the prospect, customer and consumer with even more insipid messages or trite propaganda.

Take brave steps

Have the courage to ask of your prospect, consumer and customer what marketing mix appeals to them instead of haranguing them with messages across all fronts; specifically check with them the possible permutations and let them choose. Aspire to and obtain not just their endorsement to communicate with them, but an endorsement of their best possible marketing mix. *Best by their definition, and with their permission – they chose it!*

Liberty exists in proportion to wholesome restraint; the more restraint on others to keep off from us, the more liberty we have.

DANIEL WEBSTER

Preparing, predicting and performing campaigns

12

> *Money coming in says I've made the right marketing decisions.* **ADAM OSBORNE**

Main principle

Let us start with a quick thought experiment, looking at just how many variables we have to contend with when preparing, predicting and performing campaigns (as if you needed reminding).

During my tenure as Chair of the Chartered Institute of Marketing's Technology Group, we introduced a much needed update to the traditional and principal tool of marketing – The Marketing Mix; which of course is indelibly hard-wired into the brain as the infamous and ubiquitous '4Ps' of marketing and which still resists its overdue revision to this day: *Product, Place, Promotion* and *Price.*

> *Half the money I spend on advertising is wasted, and the problem is I do not know which half.*
>
> **LORD LEVERHULME**

Short, incomplete, overly simplistic and bereft of some key fundamental and important modern marketing elements, we beefed these Ps up to the '17 Ps' – that additionally included *People* (you've got to ask yourself why this was missing from the original mix?); *Positioning* (how and where your organization and its propositions are perceived and placed within the mind of the prospect, customer or consumer); *Project Management* (as we are all managers of a number of micro and not so micro projects); *Profit* (duly described and how we measure and maintain it); *Process* (all the customer-facing, value-add activities and their corresponding methods and procedures); *Priority* (as we need to have some means to ensure that our propositions are created, improved or amended according to maximizing some weighted factors and sequence); *Policy* (the strategic protocols employed to implore and contrive us to strive towards greater consumer, customer and market centricity); *Physical Evidence* (we badly need it in marketing; truly identifying and translating customer needs to product and service propositions); *Precision* (in translating that evidence and securing defined markets); *Pervasiveness* (how marketing has influenced and penetrated our organization laterally and longitudinally); *Pleasant* (our organizations now have to be full and wholesome corporate citizens with associated good corporate governance protocols, led by marketing); *Preside* (how we are set up and governed to be better marketing-led organizations, who looks after marketing and ensures that it all works); and *Pivot* (how we actually manage to achieve a change from being seen by all as little more than 'advertising and promotions' to a more holistic and systemic process).

Phew! – *And that is just* <u>*my*</u> *17 Ps for starters.*

How about if we add all the *possible* variants to the product or service options, 'bells and whistles', the various iterations of our concepts, the possible proposition variants that the prospect, customer or consumer may wish, the branding creations and modifications, the stratagems and tactics, the promotional discounts, packages, deals, the positioning and repositioning options, the relentless onset of new disruptive technologies; the various campaigning detritus that us marketers occasionally hide behind to keep looking like we are interesting, employable people and fighting fit?

Our variables run into the *gazillions*. Yet of course, only some of these existing or potential new variables actually *matter*. At least, only a few may or can, be changed appropriately and make the most *significant* income or profit swing. That is what we wish to achieve, no less. If we achieve the same income or profit over a given period, then that is not too bad. But of course, the pressure is always on to achieve more. If you subscribe to the premise set out at the start of this book – that major changes to competitive advantage, income and profitability are at your fingertips from an insight into dealing with the true challenges in marketing – then we can and should expect to *gain a significant income or profit swing rather than just a modest improvement.*

So, what variables do we choose? In the first instance, they must come from *a firm and elegant core problem resolution,* a major priority opportunity one would aspire to exploit. The starting point can be data that forms the basis of needs identification for the prospect, customer or consumer and data that identifies the main limitations and constraints in the market and/or within our organization; and when we know what we need to know that we don't already know (as a certain high ranking American politician of recent times may have put it) then we can move on to test our proposition variables.

Easy? Not quite. In a nutshell, we need to know the priorities – the evidence-backed needs of the system. We can however check this internally and externally. In any system – or supply chain – there is only one weakest link. Start there. It is hard to find, but there are ways to do that, but that may be for another book, another time. Suffice to say that *you are looking for a core constraint similar to those articulated in this book.*

Core constraints – and I hope by the end of the book that you are sufficiently inquisitive to check for them and test them – can lead to an enlightened view of marketing, how you see the organization and how you see its place in a 'business ecosystem' (remember that a system is more than a single, linear supply chain). It also gives you an insight into which variables will *subsequently* be more important than others; but again I must reiterate that the core conflict/constraint analysis must be done. **Otherwise, we will try to change too much, or change in the wrong place with the wrong placebo 'solution' and look at too many proposition or campaigning options**

and a major income or profit swing will elude us! This is truly, where the old maxim 'garbage in – garbage out' applies.

Gather together the various ingredients – the problems in the system, the prospect, customer and consumer feedback (particularly the negatives, although you may feel they are bad for your karma, they are not when it comes to conducting core conflict analyses and subsequent variable experiments, as there is no such thing as a negative experimental result – ask an engineer or scientist if you do not believe this to be so). **What we can do now is realize that correlation is not causation; just because some changes or options seemed to have worked in the past, there is a good chance that they actually may not have been the variables that subsequently made, or will make, any real difference.** Using appropriate and robust analyses, we can construct a firm resolution to the problem of making predictions about our marketing mix permutations or a means to realize the opportunity to change them for the better. That is, we can actually manage to construct what we consider the best proposition for change and improvement – a new policy, process, orientation, or product/service PROPOSITION. If, of course, we can manage to hone down our primary mix elements that evidentially require to be changed, based on our core conflict analysis. **Imagine cutting down from literally hundreds or thousands of mix permutations to introducing *optimal changes* to only a handful of key marketing mix variables?**

Underpinning contradiction and beliefs to confront

Can your measurement and decision-making system(s) cope with your *customers'* ideas of value and *their* measurements too? Can we take all those variables, even if we have cut them down to translate the 'big breakthrough idea' that resolves a core conflict or realizes your greatest opportunity and work comprehensively and confidently, even though we still may have many variables to contend with? Can your systems and decision-making processes cope? It is certainly insufficient to simply tweak and flirt with proposition variants *ad infinitum* across all the marketing mix elements, to eventually come up with some kind of 'optimized' proposition. Earlier we discussed how there are too many variables – it would take disproportionately long, spending too much money and utilizing too many resources, to be able to test all possible configurations; and by the time you may have just about got it right, the market may have changed and the opportunity evaporates. My hope is that armed with a focusing capability to look at the core constraints and conflicts and the emergence of suitable technology, we marketers may yet develop the key to effectiveness and *corresponding* superior efficiencies in creating propositions and orchestrating campaigns. See Figure 12 for the core conflict. *(Optimizing your proposition, the marketing mix variables, is being investigated and developed as part of a major ongoing initiative – The Epsilon Project – see the Appendix for details.)*

FIGURE 12   It is all a question of returns...

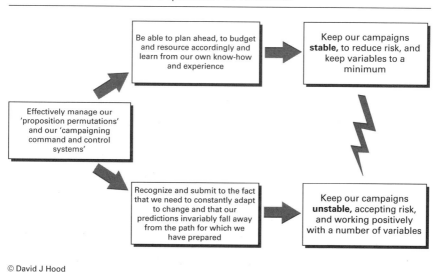

© David J Hood
The Marketing Manifesto™

Testing assumptions

1 Be able to plan ahead, to budget and resource accordingly and learn from our own know-how and experience, because:

a we need an easy way to set a budget, and to set them using a consistent process of calculating and allocating, that is easily understood by all in the organization;

b there are so many strategic and tactical options to consider; we have to plan well ahead and consolidate our activities and set budgets and targets ahead of actually knowing how we intend to respectively use and achieve them, or what challenges or opportunities may materialize for which we may have to set aside money for later;

c we need to set budgets well ahead so that cash is ring-fenced now for our important marketing activities; so budgeting and planning must all be based on historical data extrapolation of as many certainties as possible, rather than adding to an already complex set of variables;

d we are 'competing' with other activities and people within the organization for the same money; we therefore have to calculate our budget submissions in the same way as other areas of the business (with an internal focus);

e we like to keep a consistent outlay and set plan for marketing spend (eg a potential event worked for us last year, so we should do it this year too) and this allows us some stability in budget setting and expenditure, which we really like (and colleagues both like and expect this too).

Today we increasingly think in terms of qualities rather than quantities. Consumers or customers do not want more of the same, but different and better... from matter to mind.

PROF LUIZ MOUTINHO

2 **Therefore... we keep our campaigns STABLE, to reduce risk, and keep variables to a minimum, because:**

a our budgets don't really allow for changes, tweaks or unexpected modifications to costs or activities;

b we need to reduce our 'decision making options' and not add to our workload; stable budgets set at the outset that correspond with stable activities help us to reduce our load;

c we know by and large how and where to spend our budgets and it has more or less always worked out well for us in the past;

d we sadly have both a societal and a business culture where failure is deemed to be bad and success is good; so we need to tend towards stability in everything we do and be seen to be making every aspect of our operations stable;

e consistency fosters a perception of stability and a sense of assured delivery to the board and shareholder;

f instability is bad, and results in negative outputs (perceived or real campaign or product failures for instance) and less certainty all round;

g standardizing leads to efficiencies and this is liked by finance (and even perhaps by our sales colleagues).

3 **We recognize and submit to the fact that we need to constantly adapt to change and that our predictions invariably fall away from the path for which we are prepared because:**

a targets rarely work out the way we wish them to, either in monetary terms or in their timing;

b it should save us grief in its many different forms if we actually accept that change will happen and embrace it; whether we need to change, or it is imposed upon us and we have the desire and the capacity to change, be agile and try different paths and activities in *real time*, to keep up with our anticipated income requirements;

c we have to prepare ourselves for the inevitable changes that occur, many of them from 'left field';

d we will otherwise be fooled into believing our targets and assumptions are always right, things will not change and we will always meet our annual goals.

Success is transient, evanescent. The real passion lies in the poignant acquisition of knowledge about all the shading and subtleties of the creative secrets.

KONSTANTIN STANISLAVISKY

4 Therefore... we keep our campaigns UNSTABLE, accepting risk, working positively with a number of variables, because:

a we know precisely where to innovate and how; we effectively know with confidence which variables to change and which not to change (rather than tinker with 'safe' and 'stable' options *ad infinitum*);

b innovating everywhere is good – that is what the business gurus tell us, and we tell ourselves;

c competitiveness is surely linked with creative risk as it relates to trying to effectively manipulate the marketing mix to suit current and changing market dynamics;

d market and customer needs change quickly, so are inherently unstable anyway;

e instability is not necessarily bad – human or societal evolution itself is necessarily unstable? *(The fringes of any community, group or society adapt and change to effect evolution of the whole or greater part);*

f we learn a lot more from instability and variance than we do from 'retracting into our shells', playing safe or sticking to historical and 'stable tweaking';

g *managed* instability means that we can adapt and more effectively react (or even be proactive) to change.

Core conflict

It is partly a question of whether we see our marketing spend as a budget or an investment. At least, that issue (*see mini-Manifesto 5 on Finance*) supports the core conflict where we look for too much stability – or we seek it in the wrong form. What do we mean by the term and what do we want from stability? Maybe we just want the ability to predict what we need to do, what budgets we need to spend, and therefore what money we would have left over for other activities over any given period.

I have not failed. I've just found 10,000 ways that won't work.

THOMAS EDISON

But the problem is, in setting those budgets early (ie well before we need them) it will effectively 'energize' them prematurely; we then peculiarly find ourselves planning and acting based on set and quickly out-of-date figures and budget spend, rather than the need for agile action to meet market need. If we are to mature, and look at marketing spend as an investment rather than a budget item, **then we must more comprehensively embrace this instability, link it with our agility, and start planning in real time.** It is difficult for us to plan and predict, given the conflict between budget vs investment; and this particular challenge is further compounded by the conflict between 'being safe, tweaking and tinkering with the creative variables' vs 'being really innovative by finding out what variables will rapidly resolve core conflicts for us and the market and how those variables should be configured.'

WHAT to change

- The propensity to 'tactically tinker or tweak' or otherwise play with all or some of the ideas for new marketing mix variables is insufficient, inefficient, and in many cases, can be mostly *ineffective*.

- The 'ability to predict is the essence of management', yet it has to be better in terms of increasing certainty and reducing risk through improving our capability to predict.

- Variation should stymie our ability to predict; yet we *need* it – although we fight against it as we want stability. Can we actually use variation and variety to our advantage? Even if this conflicts with our core feelings, which tell us that variation is bad?

- 'Replace' the usual sales funnels with customer value and intellectual property creating, protecting and developing models.

Correlation between the data on prospect, customer or consumer need, or data on variables associated with any or all elements of the proposition – frequently does not equate to causation, yet we fall foul of this factual error constantly and consistently.

DAVID JAMES HOOD

What to change TO

- A regime of changing *only* the marketing mix elements – the variables in the proposition – that make the greatest (evidenced!) impact on the consumers' or customers' profit, experience or enjoyment, and therefore our own.

- Reduce risk, without unduly reducing the capability for real, necessary and valued *specific* innovations.

- See our results from our main marketing-related activities as positive – even those we think have yielded a negative result – and adopt a useful process technology to take account and learn from those 'experiments'.

- A developed 'pull-forward' approach and accompanying process for new product or service development (NPSD) that shortens lead times for both NPSD and time-to-impact for individual and a series of campaigns.

- A non-arbitrary way of setting and allocating marketing spend (one based on enhanced integration of real-time feedback of results and a corresponding reduction in wasted time, effort and money)!

HOW to change

- Eliminate the external core constraint (the one in the market) after eliminating our internal core constraint; but then bring the constraint back in again where possible – where we can control and address it and ensure continuous and sustainable competitive advantage.

- Know precisely where to make changes to campaigns or 'the proposition' and make that change the lead factor in innovation decisions, strategic direction and budgeting considerations.

- Use a system that learns something from what would normally be considered a 'negative' result – eg a failed campaign output/ input – and which in turn can actually learn (which of course is a positive input) from ANY result (we should always learn from any experiment).

- Introduce and invest in a budget allocation policy and process that sees marketing SOLELY as an investment, with an EXPECTED return, not simply as an expenditure item.

- Rid your lexicon and understanding of marketing of the notion of 'governance through and in accordance with arbitrance' and change to 'governance through evidential marketing' that subsequently informs the decisions regarding what variables of the marketing mix should and would be manipulated for change and improvement.

Reflection and action

How often have we heard ourselves or others say 'when we look back at our strategy (or tactics/campaigns), we did not achieve "x", so we did "y", and it all worked out OK'? Granted, we changed some variable or variables along the way, but we never checked back or changed why, how and what we actually *measured at that time*. We tend to assume that our measurement methods are correct. I am proposing not just a change in how we measure campaigns and marketing mix variables, but how we then go on to try to maximize our outputs accordingly.

We do have a tendency to examine the issues and snippets of information that conform to and confirm our current understanding or existing knowledge, not our ignorance. We also understandably tend to look for a positive result in what we do – at least a result that seems to conform to our output expectations or may validate them. We can be somewhat forgiven in this as we do desire to drive successful campaigns, back to back, to keep on track and realize our important revenue targets; but this clouds our vision somewhat regarding the nature and opportunity of appropriately testing and experimenting with proposition variables. Again this is understandable, but we do lose so much thanks to our basic assumption that any negative result – ie those tweaks or activities that do not have the desired effect – are somewhat considered as failures. We can and should learn from those 'failures', but we traditionally consider and assess them only as failures, and as such we overlook an excellent opportunity to learn (that much perhaps is obvious) and to realize that even negative results are positive if handled and viewed properly. *As said earlier, a good engineer will tell you that there is no such thing as a negative result…* this is known as the 'silent evidence' of so-called negative results. So do we therefore look for greater stability, to supposedly make it easier to plan, budget ahead and ready the organization based on stable propositions and annual timeframes that force us to budget and allocate for a forward period of time; OR will we seek to be proactive, operating in real time, and take the challenges and opportunities presented by the dynamics of the market that impact us and correspondingly act with recourse only to real-time return on investment calculations instead?

Could we be detracted because we are looking to achieve what I call 'unstable stability' rather than accepting and embracing 'stable instability'? (See the following mini-Manifesto on Corporate Governance and Turnaround for more on that issue.) Organizations and business thinking have always favoured attempts to make the unstable stable; unstable stability is the traditional approach that attempts to take instabilities, tame them, and reduce them to a 'stable state' – thus throttling the organization's ability to be agile. Organizations that have a *self-centric* rather than a customer or market-centric orientation conform markedly to this approach. *Stable instability* however, seeks to embrace the fact that instability is good; a virtue indeed from living in a complex multi-connected and multi-faceted world instead of seeking to tame it. This does not involve taking leave of your senses, suspending disbelief, or adopting some random initiative that involves encouraging too many variables; it specifically means reducing those variables, not taming nor limiting them. Stable instability relishes the instability so necessary for agility and constant and consistent improvement as we rapidly change to address the smaller number of key, well-defined and focused variables.

Take brave steps

Assess how you can move from an annual budgeting and planning system to one that works in **real time**. This does not mean you suspend or discontinue your *forward* planning, your strategizing with timeframes and sensing and preparing for the future. What I mean here is that your sense and respond system has to be created or improved in keeping with the kind of sense and respond capability you would wish your organization to actually have. **To put it another way, the longer it takes to set your planning and budgeting and the more detailed your future spend and limitations placed on how any investment will be spent, and the longer the period that it covers and is set, (it *will* be pretty much set in stone when it was agreed, with little adjustment or wriggle room available for you to change or be sufficiently agile) then the longer your organization will take to react to any given market forces.** You could call that *'Marketing's Third Law of Motion'*.

Develop a means to pull in the time taken to 'test' possible or probable propositions with differing mix or variants; perform iterative tests on key configurations, driving the marketing mix to an optimum. A situation of stable instability. Evidentially know which variations link best with resolutions of conflicts or limitations within your business sphere. Of course, the answer is not so clear cut. The core conflict demonstrates why we think there are very good reasons for stability in budgeting, in defining marketing activities from the outset, and in tweaking through changes to the marketing mix. We need to address both sides of the conflict – that much is clear. Can we find a breakthrough, without having to compromise? Can we develop the smart process technology and capabilities that will allow us to have 'stable instability', giving us enhanced opportunity and wealth from a new ability to invest where we need to quickly make immediate changes to the proposition; so that we no longer play safe, resolutely refusing to have to fight the frenzy of 'annual posturing and morsel-mongering' that invariably mimimizes budgets; turn away now from the let's-do-more-of-the-same-as-we-did-last-quarter, and learn unashamedly from *all* our ongoing marketing campaigning experiences?

> *True stability results when presumed order and presumed disorder are balanced. A truly stable system expects the unexpected, is prepared to be disrupted, and waits to be transformed.*
>
> **TOM ROBBINS**

Integrating marketing into an invigorated corporate governance

13

Main principle

Accepted Good Corporate Governance (GCG) tenets tend not to include marketing strategy, effectiveness or management of marketing's component activities. Apart from the use of some 'non-specific niceties' and some marketing-related issues that come under general activities and terms such as 'audit' and 'understanding risks', most GCG structures, protocols, deeds and policies tend to focus on the primary accounting, reporting and fiscal disclosure requirements and legal and commercial obligations to shareholders and the expectations of political and governmental authorities.

Take a look at any company end-of-year report, or top-level management briefing to their shareholders or owners. An interesting experiment would be to scan through a few of those reports and look at the importance placed on marketing; check for an incidence or any mention of the customer in those lovely, glossy brochures of so little use yet that are so beloved by 'corporates'. At best, you may find some mention of 'markets' that specifically offers some description of the industry sector to which the organization belongs (but not the dynamics and marketing nuances that affect and are affected within market segments). And it will be difficult to find any decent insight there either into customers, markets, competitiveness or anything that really demonstrates that the organization has a good handle on the business ecosystem, confidence in its direction or management or whether the latter is currently 'fit for purpose'.

If we don't think it worthy to report marketing issues to all our stakeholders, or give marketing a significantly high profile within GCG reporting protocols, then we could be said to be indifferent about marketing and the customer – and therefore indifferent about marketing's place of import to the organization and its governance. Marketing is not even included in recognized international quality process standards! So why should we be surprised that it is not at the top of the agenda or included in what we recognize as corporate governance.

Underpinning contradiction and beliefs to confront

Marketing is rarely *considered* – by business, but especially by the public at large – as a virtuous activity that benefits society. By extension, it is *believed* perhaps only to benefit business, usually big business, and certainly not the customer or consumer. It is understandable then that marketing is rarely seen as a probable source of positive contributions to corporate social responsibility and governance. *Everyone – including the organization and arguably its board – sees it simply as a costly, necessary evil.* But surely all – the process of marketing all the way through from the ability to identify need to delivery and beyond – would be organized, structured and operated in accordance with the wishes of, and to the benefit of all people; and good corporate governance and social responsibility would ensure all strategic, management and operational activities are in concert and meet common goals that are obviously inextricably and directly linked within a MARKET context, not isolated in a vacuum?

Surely top level management *should know better* and realize that marketing, **as something that is expected to bring in the money, needs** to be a full and integral part of good corporate governance. Everything is linked within our marketplace. Everything and everyone. If marketing was accepted as a central plank of the business – and seen as a strategic input, in both directional as well as financial terms – perhaps sales and marketing forecasts, rather than being seen as outputs, would be managed, agreed and delivered as befits any major organizational investment. Sales and marketing forecasts not only assume or confer the appearance of certainty (or rather are a representation of what the organization thinks that we can achieve) but as targets come from corporate governance rather than the market, it is assumed that corporate targets are the objective of the system (ie including all actors, from suppliers through to the final customer), although it patently is not – it is just the wishes, no more, of a certain few people within it.

Let's face it, our target figures in any given period are really finger in the air calculations at best (convince me otherwise) but we take them as 'gospel'; and likewise we treat budgets that we set to achieve those heady targets in the same deluded fashion. If we base our goals, objectives and our measurements on fatuous targets, with correspondingly unfounded budgeting policies and calculations, how can we be expected to be taken seriously and really help top management improve and <u>perfect</u> corporate governance?

> *Surely the best way to confidently build trust and integrity is to operate within a wholesome systemic marketing process.*

DAVID JAMES HOOD

Does financial or corporate governance and reporting actually convey anything that investors or others actually find interesting? Does it really demonstrate the health of the organization effectively, never mind providing information that may actually offer stakeholders a useful insight into our preferred and maybe ambitious direction for the way ahead? Does it confer confidence to anyone that some person with a talented team is at the helm, firmly and surely, and there is a good chance the organization will chart its way capably through uncharted, challenging waters? Doesn't corporate governance – and all our stakeholders – deserve better than 'these are our figures, and we think they are achievable' whilst strangely offering little foundation as to why those figures are what they are, and finally show a bit more confidence that **our investments in marketing and budgets are more than just a form of theatre?** I am sure that I would rather have a stakeholder or shareholder report (all reports, not just the 'annual paperback novel') that offer more than some sterile reporting figures, but actually give me an insight into how the organization is 'striving to thrive', what, why, where, who, when, which, and how. Likewise, as a shareholder (as opposed to perhaps 'just' a stakeholder) I would like to see more than corporate blurb-speak and be offered some real evidence of insight and not just capability but ACTION. The illustration in Figure 13 makes a case that **structure and hierarchy** are the defining underpinning factors in the core conflict dilemma that prevents us utilizing marketing at the topmost echelon of business – that of the 'theatre of orchestrated corporate governance'.

FIGURE 13 Why is marketing and the customer not centre stage in terms of governance?

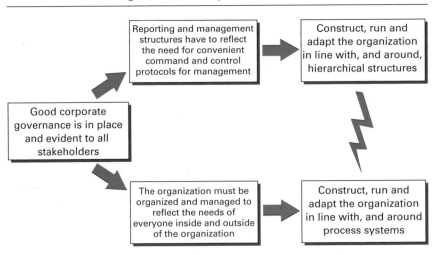

Testing assumptions

1 Reporting and management structures have to reflect the need for convenient command and control protocols for management, because:

   a we must demonstrate to all that we can control the organization's functions, at both board and senior management level;

   b everyone needs a rigid framework within which to work to make sure all tasks are orchestrated in the organization;

   c it is the 'corporate way', and everything is run on 'reports about reports and meetings' and internal moving, shaking and 'politicking';

   d top level management is where the decisions are made, where the taps are turned on or off, from where the 'troops are manoeuvred';

   e those who own our organization, and correspondingly those we have to report to, expect us to have hierarchies and related reporting structures that reflect and effect 'command and control' and 'city' type requirements of running a business.

There is less to fear from outside competition than from inside inefficiency, discourtesy and bad service.

ANONYMOUS

2 Therefore... we construct, run and adapt the organization in line with, and around hierarchical structures, because:

   a constant alignment and realignment of strategy, goals, objectives, tactics and campaigning needs constant command and control structure involvement to manage and disseminate any and all information, resources and material flows;

   b a rigid structure helps us keep some degree of continuity in the face of relentless change, external forces and changes in personnel and resources;

c 'departmentalization' always allows for the convenient development of specificity and organizing resources in the most efficient way, and has always been the best way to control people and their functions;

d it is easier to manage, finance, resource and measure those discrete resources and activities around and through functional units, and marketing is no exception.

3 **The organization must be organized and managed to reflect the needs of everyone inside and outside the organization because:**

a stakeholders are a large group of people, both inside and outside of the organization, and their needs must be met in concert; but not to the detriment of one or more parties whether they are internal or external to the organization;

b we have an obligation to others, not just to our own defined roles or 'bosses' within the organization; we know that not everything can 'go through' the obligatory 'corporate conduit' and be discussed, agreed and processed 'through in and out trays' otherwise we will be less than agile;

c we need to keep everyone appropriately involved and informed and therefore must ensure we communicate with all stakeholders in the most effective and meaningful way;

d our interactions internally and externally through tangible and intangible means, must support the process of conducting business, not some abstract hierarchy. Far too often, we find that we serve a hierarchy 'just because it is there' rather than it serving us. This is outdated and restricts our scope for matching needs with resources, for profit.

4 **Therefore... we construct, run and adapt the organization in line with, and around process systems, because:**

a as with the human body, the thing that keeps our organization healthy and alive are the connections and communications between the individual components, and not simply the structures employed;

b it is PROCESSES that give us the ability to create and manage corporate governance outputs (eg dashboard, corporate governance financial data etc) so it should be a process that handles the key inputs, especially the ones that result in the corresponding figures to do with markets: needs, research and development, prospecting, orders, income, profit etc – the marketing inputs and outputs;

c a process can communicate between all functions, people and activities, whereas a physical hierarchy arguably cannot do so as readily, transparently and with consistency (and without bias, or some self-seeking intent or other agenda);

d *we are all customers of each other and are all performing exchanges* – therefore we need a marketing process system that can accommodate all the information and tangible or intangible exchanges that are required to be passed around; something that people cannot do by themselves in this age of information overload; we need a process system that ensures that the good of the system prevails (and provides a checking mechanism against any undue forces and conflicting agendas that bedevil all organizations due in large part to their hierarchical architecture and resulting 'compounded fiefdoms' and singular worldviews).

Core conflict

What we have here is a general conflict, in that it is not only marketing and the marketer that could be aided by a fundamental change from a hierarchical structure to a process-based one; but marketing IS a process and set of activities, not a department or a function; so in finally recognizing this anomaly and changing this situation, the organization can really give their marketing and competitive prowess a major boost.

WHAT to change

- Reliance on *standard* governance measurements: the 'city reporting' and reporting mechanisms to the organization's publics and shareholders – what we are 'expected to do' – but this does not truly and effectively reflect the wealth or health of the company, its ongoing opportunity development, **real value improvement and delivery,** nor sufficiently reflects or informs the best course or path to take now and in the future.

- A lack of policies and frameworks to see and develop employees and colleagues as key competitive advantage resources in their own right.

- The reliance on cost controlling as THE focus for management decisions – doing so seems safer, easier, more comfortable, more obvious and *visible* – but it actually IMPEDES the possibility of great delivery to the customer or consumer.

Never treat your audience as customers, always as partners.

JIMMY STEWART

- The obsession with top level 'governance by impedance' that appears to – and does – prohibit real innovation or at best reduces empowerment to act in any way other than conforming to the behaviour that is universally accepted in the organization and conforms to the existing top-down measurements that are in place. **This is seen in the widely experienced problem of management inertia causing major constraints in the system; such as various policies and protocols, authorizing activities, progressing developmental projects through iterative meetings and many other instances of impedance, inertia and rank neglect of certain functional components of the organization.**

- Using synthetic corporate 'stability aligners' that seek to reign in and succeed in keeping the organization 'stuck in same' – giving the *appearance and impression* of stable governance and prognosis for a healthy future (such as those exposed in recent cases of corporate fraud – that continue to manifest themselves in poor or less-than-clear corporate reporting and management).

- Do not have your organization creating or providing things that people – prospects, customers or consumers – will not buy (or readily buy)! Obvious – but it is happening all around you, everywhere.

- The limitations placed on you, by the market and 'competitive forces'. This is key to GCG and will really make your shareholders sit up and applaud the true integration of marketing into a reinvigorated corporate governance.

What to change TO

- Set up meaningful 'dashboards' measuring values as a calibration point rather than measurements that are a product of cost, cost accounting (or cost + margin etc).

- Improve *market* capitalization by increasing *human* intellectual capitalization by increasing human *intellectual property* capital, not decreasing it – creating a virtuous cycle of competitiveness.

- Reset your measurements and aspirations – check some of your own assumptions as to what the organizational and system goals are; how these goals and the business system is best measured systemically rather than simply by unit sale or other prevailing methodologies (see *mini-Manifesto 5*).

- Measurements are the force that guides the system – change them to focus on marketing-based knowledge acquisition and deployment mechanisms, processes and activities.

- Decisions on developed, prioritized opportunities for improvement and change are made with confidence.

- A culture is fostered and nurtured of 'developed, (evolved) stable instability' and get everyone in the organization excited about it. (See earlier *Manifesto 12* for a short discussion on stable instability.)

- A 'zero-waste' attitude prevails – and is set in concrete at board level (*after all, having our system creating and delivering things that the prospect, customer or consumer actually needs must make sense at the board level and offers the 'path of least resistance to profit'*).

- Eliminate the market constraint (the reason that the market is not buying with a degree of sufficiency, or there is an overcapacity in the market/system that may also lead to the same outcome). Eliminating constraints, methodologically, one by one, provides a priority for change... Imagine offering GCG Reports that inform about the **destruction of ongoing major conflicts and constraints** rather than simple and vacuous words about corporate tinkering with figures and other reportage babble?

HOW to change

- Integrate marketing processes (especially sense and respond systems) fully into the centre of the development of Intellectual Capital (all resources that determine the value and the competitiveness of an enterprise): namely research and development (Structural Intellectual Capital), people, process and systems (Human Capital) and currently developed and future product and service or so-called Brand Equity (Customer-Market Capital, including systemic relationships).

- Develop brand/customer advocates that PULL your products and services into the market based on need and desire, rather than *pushing* to the market using internal measurements and unfounded targets.

- Rip up standard policies and processes that use received wisdom about corporate governmental measurements and how to improve by using them (they don't work properly).

- Stop the 'Rabid Centrifugality' to upper management and the board and replace with mobile, transitory 'prioritized agility points' (PAPs) – which could be managed by the marketer throughout the organization and beyond – that ensure the optimum service from the marketing, value and innovation activities and which determine overall prioritization for any improvements to the organization.

- Resign yourself to the notion that stability is not definitive, and is wholly arbitrary. Markets change, customers change, and customer need changes... Almost everything changes. Your intuition holds that 'the market' is the rudder guiding your ship – **reflect that in your corporate government measurements, reporting input and outputs,** and from that realize real agility and competitiveness!

- Only make or create things that your prospects, customers or consumers want to buy (a few current management thinkers could be said to be behind the notion of less-is-more, such as Gladwell, Goldratt, and Nassim Nicholas Taleb; they suggest that we check and challenge the notion and momentum to innovate everywhere and make all kinds of changes to propositions instead of focusing on the areas and issues that *matter* – making life intuitively easier for many, including the marketer).

- Bring the market constraint INSIDE the business (ie the market would wish to buy a proposition that we have conceptualized, but that we are unable to bring to them appropriately due to some internal problem, conflict, or limitation) and resource up excess capacity to break that constraint and serve it – elevating and capitalizing on that constraint. (It behoves the marketer to ensure excess capacity exists within the organizational system to meet peak and additional loads on the system and in the *extremely likely* case that 'Murphy's Law' happens – the unforeseen crisis that happens more often than we care to remember!)

- An organization is a living human system, itself part of a greater living system – and is therefore not a faceless corporation; it is this reassessment coupled with an aspiration for a deeper understanding of this certainty that is a prerequisite to fully achieving competitive sustainability and to being able to adapt to the constant need for change and the tenet of significantly developing Good Corporate Governance.

Tell me how you will measure me, and I will tell you how I will behave. If my measurements are not clear, no one can predict how I will behave, not even me.

DR ELI GOLDRATT

Reflection and action

'Quality' is not just a department. Nor is 'IT'; their *presence, use* and *penetration* is everywhere in the organization. Our corporate financial systems are likewise. (For instance, the latter are linked to sales and operational systems.) Administration is not confined to some defined Administration department – we all do *some*. These are all examples of corporate silos that have broken out, as they had to permeate the entire organization and beyond to work effectively and to better correspond with those business and operational elements required for inputs and outputs. Anything that is seen to help the flow around, in and out of the organization is arguably practically owned by everyone. We are all responsible for 'quality' and some shared objectives. However, not all staff are currently responsible for marketing... It is high time for marketing to 'come out from the cupboard under the stairs' or down from its ivory tower... *It is marketing's turn to break out.*

... **And it is marketing's turn to *run* the organization.**

Take brave steps

- Realize that the goal is not *unstable stability* – it is actually *stable instability*: the former is reactive and the latter proactive; the former is fire fighting to keep things the same, the latter realizing that everything is constantly changing and we can use this to our advantage.

- Exterminate budget-setting practices for marketing and replace with an Investment Response Model (IRM) to proactively translate customer needs and test our delivery; this leads to greater agility, better response to changes in the market, and also **does away with the WEEKS and MONTHS of budgetary planning** by moving to real time capabilities and saving money whilst doing so.

- Good Corporate Governance starts and ends with the market, so reflect that reality properly and appropriately in structures, processes, management and reporting.

- Grasp the 'governance thistle' – it isn't as thorny as you'd expect – and realize that there is a total lack of congruence or alignment between high level governance and the 'coal face' that is the market and its requirements and needs.

- Put marketing at the heart of your strategy to attain Good Corporate Governance – have the marketing process govern the organization as a 'listening, caring and prioritizing guiding hand' **because marketing BRINGS IN THE MONEY.**

This is an era in which corporations want to be lily white because corporate governance is on the front burner.

HOWARD DAVIDOWITZ

Corporate mergers, acquisitions and turnarounds (CMAT): where the hell is marketing?

14

If you fire people, you fire customers. **FERDINAND PIECH**

Main principle

Every day in the business pages of the quality news or business media on and offline, we read of companies and organizations that are under some severe strain; many such organizations are reportedly going or have gone through a merger, acquisition or attempted some kind of 'turnaround' (which I collectively call CMAT).

We see there is a major dynamic in business where at the highest level, stresses and strains abound in relation to strategic change of a magnitude that perhaps has never been seen in those organizations before the reported crisis or crises hit them.

We read or hear about (or indeed unfortunately are on the receiving end of some hard and unpleasant experience of) the usual 'corporate dancing'; where representatives of the respective organizations are wheeled out, to face the great and the good, the media hacks and chattering classes, and presumably the shareholders (and a few other stakeholders), to 'inform' all of the situation along with earnest assurances that the 'best is being done' to get out of the predicament.

> *Marketing is distilling chaos into beauty.*
>
> **MEG SMITH**

And what is being done? The usual awful paraphernalia of crises: internal jousting, financial 'jiggery', swinging and scything cuts, new heads coming in, old heads rolling, deadwood chipped, consolidations galore, numbers crunched and lovely new portfolios and structures created and supposedly ugly ones destroyed. And of course, a picturesque reshuffle and usurpation resulting in the movement of people who were probably doing a pretty good job and who probably should have been left to do it.

Every stratagem and tactic employed in CMAT seems to result in another proverbial and significant 'nail in the coffin of excellence' for the organization; with every so-called merger, acquisition or turnaround appearing to involve short term knee-jerk 'solutions' (oh, how I hate the pejorative and ubiquitous use of that 'solutions' word), that create vaporous 'improvements' that are invariably short lived – and short sighted. Within those very significant strategic changes to organizations, where the hell is marketing? Where the hell is the customer? When organizations are stressed, yes, their collective backs may be to the wall, but the board and senior management should not be facing it too! *They have to look outwards as well.*

> *Business continuity is becoming a major issue for companies of all sizes. The message is finally getting through; any company that is prepared to risk letting their customers down or gamble with the needs of their employees is going to pay a heavy penalty at some time – we need a comprehensive platform where we can learn about solutions in this vitally important area.*
>
> **JOHN SHARP**

Underpinning contradiction and beliefs to confront

I have argued elsewhere in this book that we have to face up to a vicious and pernicious attitude and reliance on the evil twins of cost-cutting and cost-accounting. These twins are ever evident when a CMAT situation is being faced.

Cost cutting could be said to inadvertently (or with full knowledge) cause a reduction in the organization's Intellectual Capital, its 'know-how' that cannot be codified or truly calculated (*of course, talent does not appear on balance sheets, so it is maybe a case of 'what the hell'*).

When such a major change is envisaged or being undertaken, I am struck as to why no one is looking out for the component parts of the organization and business that matter the most in terms of continuity and improvement: the consumer, the customer, the prospect, our people (all are creators and providers of value after all), the market, the products and services, the marketing mix and **everything that actually brings in the money.**

Of course, very little real attention is given at the top level of the organization to TRUE business continuity – pleasuring the consumer or customer and ensuring that front-line delivery is definitely NOT adversely affected!

It is striking to witness that during times of major change and turnaround, just how little is known by senior management (or their advisors) about the organization's range of products and services, processes, procedures or the key sources of Intellectual Capital or competitive advantage. What is proposed here is that the underlying conflict is preventing us becoming a bit more adventurous and taking a rare opportunity to get everyone involved in a change for the better – for the creators, providers and users of 'value'. Indeed any change should be an occasion to improve delivery to the consumer or customer – even during a stressful CMAT situation!

Instead of cutting back and drawing in – what about delivering almost the opposite? Our people and our customers, the two most important entities, would be right on our side if at corporate level we were to instigate a process of RESOURCING rather than cutting back; and in the case of acquisitions and mergers, we would surely be in a situation where we have additional people to allow us to free up some capacity. Resist the urge to prescribe, or be party to, a corporate crash diet! This is a big wow if we think about it clearly. Because, after all, you will probably reflect and see the irony that the excuse 'we do not have sufficient resources' has surely impeded our ability to initiate and realize a whole plethora of ambitions over previous years! Figure 14 illustrates the question of cuts versus excess capacity. No excuses exist now... you may suddenly have the resources to turn what can be a stressful situation into a wonderful opportunity to really turn things around for the better – and for the long term.

> *If we keep doing what we're doing, we're going to keep getting what we're getting.*
>
> **DR STEPHEN R COVEY**

FIGURE 14 Leveraging marketing to effect major corporate change...

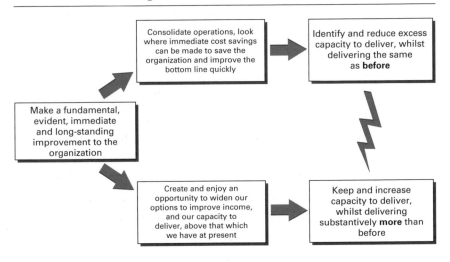

© David J Hood
The Marketing Manifesto™

Testing assumptions

1 **Consolidate operations, look where immediate cost savings can be made to save the organization and improve the bottom line quickly, because:**

   a there is an expectation that the loss of cash and shareholder value must be arrested;

   b cost savings can readily and painlessly be made;

    c cost savings can actually save the organization or induce a radical, sustainable and *robust* improvement to the bottom line;

    d it is a quick and simple measure to save some money;

    e it is the cost side of the equation that is likely to be wrong – not the market or income side.

2 Therefore... identify and reduce excess capacity to deliver, whilst delivering the same as before, because:

    a we can cut and trim down yet again, as we have excess capacity;

    b we need to ensure that our delivery ability does not suffer unduly;

    c our customers are all happy with the level of service that they currently have and we cannot nor need not improve upon it;

    d cost cutting is the best way to improve quickly as an organization as we can easily identify and implement savings;

    e we are confident that when we carved off what we thought we didn't need in the past, this proved to be the most important way to cut costs, regardless of what will be a very different and perhaps difficult future ahead;

    f cost cutting is synonymous with getting rid of the fat in the business and means that we will come through leaner and fitter than before; after the major CMAT period of change.

The problems we have today cannot be solved by thinking the way we thought when we created them.

ALBERT EINSTEIN

3 Create and enjoy the opportunity to widen our options to improve income and our capacity to deliver, above that which we have at present because:

    a there is a marked opportunity for some unprecedented and more complete change due to the increased stress on us all; and as everyone's immediate focus is on the need for smooth transition and improvement, they will more likely grasp and be fully *behind the change*; especially if it means fighting our way out rather than adopting defeatist rearguard actions and saving our own individual position and circumstance that will otherwise unavoidably and sadly overtake us all;

b everyone is keen to embrace the new challenge and efforts to achieve continuity of income for themselves and the organization – if they demonstrably see that what is proposed and enacted is virtuously improving their circumstance and their ability to deliver;

c People will generally wish to 'work themselves out of a hole' rather than be pushed right into it; and they do not wish to see their colleagues suffer unduly likewise;

d we have cut all the costs we can *already – circumstances are palpably tough as things stand –* and therefore we don't wish to further harm our ability to deliver; and we would rather increase the scope of our abilities to deliver as an organization.

"*What is right is often hidden by what is convenient.*

BODIE THOENE

4 Therefore... keep and increase capacity to deliver, whilst delivering substantively more than before, because:

a the customer, consumer or prospect *always* suffers when major change is being undertaken, especially as it isn't something that they wished or asked us to do; and we need to counter this with all efforts and resources that we can deploy;

b customers may be aware of the changes we are going through and they will correspondingly scrutinize our delivery more carefully and will be more sensitive to any downward change to their perceived level of service, satisfaction or experience, or any kind of bad news from the market, peer groups, or commentators; there is a clear and present danger that the market will 'play safe' and switch to our competitors;

c any change involves many hiccups along the way, so we *need* extra capacity to pick up those problems and attend to them; we additionally need a new 'stress relief taskforce'; this would be used to identify and attack a small set of new conflicts and constraints or any side-effects of the CMAT change;

d in difficult times, the prospect, consumer, customer, markets and all stakeholders need a greater level of communication and delivery than ever before – that much at least is very clear;

e delivering more brings in more money now and in the future, so this could only bring good news, when we badly need it; and it offers a better prognosis and perception for enhanced, longer term organizational health and sustainability;

f the competition will not anticipate our move (indeed they will of course be prophesying our demise as they think we will be following the conventional path).

Core conflict

In our efforts to make a swift turnaround, we forget what we are turning around. **We are not turning around a short-term profit and loss *account*; we are turning around what is a human-based commercial delivery system.** We also get confused between short-term sales planning that tries to help improve immediate income and strategic marketing that aims to secure current *and* future income; at best we only attempt the former. Moreover, we do this by focusing on narrow and wrongful measurements that are only useful for retrospective historical analyses whilst wielding a scythe through the business. This is all of little use for real-time steering of the corporate helm and we head our ship onto the proverbial rocks. A CMAT instance is a time to do *more*, not less.

WHAT to change

- The incredulous insistence on using brainpower and resources on activities 'skimming, slimming and stifling' the organization *that is already stressed* or undergoing major trauma!

- The outdated and ill-founded singular measurement of success for CMAT that is one year's improvement to profit (by lowering costs) on the company's books.

- Traditional balance-sheet quantitative measurements to gauge the extent of the problem and especially, using these to deliver options for improvement.

- The bizarre propensity for blanket adherence and use of traditional, simplistic historical regressive data from previous years, that have always been used for 'tried and tested' or sector-based improvement initiatives (even though each year is markedly different to any other!).

What to change TO

- A focus on where continuing and new value is created; and vitally resisting wielding the CMAT scythe as some misplaced and perverse agent of destruction.

- Get the CMAT 'agents of change' people that you have identified or retained to identify, manage and facilitate change, OUT of the boardroom (where they most certainly like to be as they feel important, comfortable and worthy there) and INSIDE the value development and delivery process and have them sit, literally, with the prospect, customer or consumer.

- Adopting a new word-of-mouth based 'primer paradigm' to measure word of mouth (WOM) as a base point for rapid improvement from where we currently are pre-CMAT; make sure that the market knows about sincere, positive developments and manage and enjoy the associated word-of-mouth activity.

- Improve only where improvements will make a profound, real and major swing to profit for BOTH the organization and the consumer or customer. (If the latter only, fine. The former should follow.)

HOW to change

- Untie the chains and shackles of the past that bind you to the usual destructive accountancy approach to CMAT.

- Start, run with and end with, the customer-consumer value chain and IGNORE cost cutting – any company in a CMAT situation has probably cut all it can (you know this to be innately true – cost cutting does not earn you anything but staff and customer or consumer animosity); resource up rather than down.

- Employ a scoring, calibration and value improvement system based on true WOM measurement and *active* management of that WOM.

- Instigate a market/customer/consumer culture standardized model throughout the organization; rapidly create a 'marketing as process' or process-based marketing management (PBM^2) model based on the above tenets, and create a CMAT standard that includes and is centred around the creation of a new 'mafia offer' for customers and consumers – one they cannot refuse (because it is SO good; more on mafia offers in the web resources). *That is the way to CMAT success.* Instead of paring right back, take care and surprise and delight existing and potential customers or consumers at a time *when they least expect it*. And then watch as the competition suffers...

Sharks have been swimming the oceans unchallenged for thousands of years; chances are the species that roams corporate waters will prove just as hard.

ERIC GELMAN

Reflections and action

Recognize a constant complaint is that we never have sufficient resources to deliver as we would wish. *Cutting resources is the last thing we should do, and is therefore the last refuge for the scoundrel with an impoverished mind.* Cutting is somewhat easy to *decide* to do; any organization that tries to cut where cuts cannot be made or should never have been made is not innovative, healthy, nor was it anywhere near the best place to start to effect a seamless corporate merger, acquisition or turnaround. **A true turnaround or such major change needs more.**

Improvements need more. If you have the resources, then do not cut them, as they will always be working up around full capacity anyway. That is the simple law of physics – you can call it Marketing's second law of Corporate Dynamics, that states that 'Every organization will sweat to the absolute limit, the wholly available capacity from every resource within the organization, as anything less is seen as inefficient'. Ask any finance person if you wish to substantiate this... Anyway, the point is that there just is nothing left to cut. In a CMAT situation, they will be expected to do more, with less, and if the grim reaper of cuts gets his or her way, everyone will have to do it with a *lot* less.

> *Surely strategy when it comes to corporate mergers, acquisitions and turnarounds should be more than just adopting the usual policies of collateral damage used to improve figures in the short term, coupled with a scorched earth policy towards everything.*
>
> **DAVID JAMES HOOD**

Let us look instead to marketing to get us out of the hole and propel us into sustainable financial and competitive health.

Take brave steps

- Resource UP – ensure that there is excess capacity – going through a difficult change means that the prospect, the customer or consumer, the market, the partner, are all going to be put out by the changes that inevitably have to be made. By resourcing up *instead* of down the customer or consumer will be pleasantly surprised and will give your position within the market a huge fillip and bolster and grow your advantage at a time when it surely will go the other way if you adopted the usual policy of 'presiding over the creation of major collateral damage and associated scorched earth' that happens during CMAT.

- **Realize that what you perceive – or will perceive – as 'growth' is not what it should be.** Challenge your assumptions – what do you wish from 'growth'? What do you really want from your CMAT exercise?

  Once you have tested these assumptions and firmed up what you mean by 'growth', drill that down to some meaningful objectives, as growth – for the sake of it, or how it is usually defined – is not the objective.

  'Growth' is a means to an end, not an end in itself; and there are many ways to define and configure to 'grow' other than in the classic sense – the strange but understandable, though unedifying, corporate race towards eating up as much of the proverbial and ethereal market. (And of course not realizing that most markets resist 'growth' and the growth required to increase that market or share of market is limited to the confines of planet Earth. Or is that 'planet Reality' perhaps?)

  The use of the usual and inappropriate definitions for 'growth' limits the boundaries that surround the mind; limiting markets, limiting aspirations, limiting your own and organizational goals to the finite constraints that exist in your market and the norms of corporate expectations – **indeed it actually limits the scope for the organization to understand the needs of the customer** (as it thinks it knows them and acts accordingly, oblivious to why it isn't achieving targets nor enjoying much of a competitive advantage).

I mentioned early on that I recognize there are hurdles, and we're going to achieve those hurdles.

GEORGE W BUSH

- An organization is surely an effective and efficient means to deliver propositions – but only if we are creating and maintaining consistent delivery of strong, highly competitive and relevant propositions, rather than focusing on the needs of some bricks and mortar self-serving entity or 'city' institutions.

- Move to a 'rolling sales pipeline' management style and process rather than obsessing about keeping to projected quarterly sales targets (this is an interesting concept and one for further debate within our profession, engaging with our fellow professionals in sales. I have begun to address this issue in my book 'Competitive SME').

In taking an *abundance* approach to change rather than a *scarcity* approach, you will get the buy-in from your people and others (including potential and existing customers or consumers)... it is a straight choice between:

1 **Abundance:** excess capacity, seizing renewal, inclusive spirit, delivery as before or better;

2 **Scarcity**: tightening belts, scorched earth policy, individual fighting, poorer delivery and a *worsening* competitive situation.

> *Marketing takes a day to learn. Unfortunately it takes a lifetime to master.*
>
> **PHILIP KOTLER**

The answer lies in including and positioning marketing central stage in your corporate mergers, acquisitions and turnarounds. Exclude marketing if you will, it is your gamble. It is everyone's loss.

...You choose!

> *Every so-called corporate merger, acquisition or turnaround appears to involve short-term knee-jerk reactions, creating vaporous 'improvements' that are invariably short lived, short sighted and short on value.*
>
> **DAVID JAMES HOOD**

Marketing leadership: it is time to step up to the mark

15

Management is doing things right; leadership is doing the right things. PETER DRUCKER

Main principle

Corporate or organizational marketing leadership starts with personal marketing leadership. The marketer needs to act the leader, not the follower, as they should have the best perspective and under-standing of the prospect, customer or consumers' unadulterated and undeniable needs and wants and how they will be translated into valuable goods and services. The position of the marketer should be firm and unassailable.

Moreover, unlike many other issues or decisions to be made in business life, we marketers should be building overriding evidence for everything we do and what the organization should do in turn.

Leadership is said to be about inspiring and acting – demonstrating to others the direction towards a worthy purpose and how best to get there. The marketer needs to be liberated sufficiently to do just that and tool themselves up with the necessary capabilities to lead from the front. We cannot really lead from a desk behind a closed door in a marketing department (closed in the physical as well as the spiritual and metaphorical sense!).

If the marketer and the marketing process are in any way stymied from this purpose, then the corporation or organization is arguably markedly reducing the ability of the person or people best placed to lead profitability, longevity and competitive sustainability. How can we fail to do the right things, if we champion the customer who after all gives us *the revenue to run our businesses* and pay all our personal incomes?

> *If I have seen farther than others, it is because I was standing on the shoulders of giant customers and consumers.*
>
> **ISSAC NEWTON, MARKETING RESEARCHER**

Underpinning contradiction and beliefs to confront

We must adopt 'aggressive listening' of the customer, consumer and prospect, and translate that sufficiently into priority actions for the company.

'Aggressive' as many other thoughts, initiatives, notions, and other issues or activities can take us away from the goal of serving more, better, quicker and more valuable than we did before. Moreover, of course, this aggressive listening could be extended to our colleagues – our 'internal customers' as well.

There are of course many dimensions and options to gain and exhibit excellence in marketing leadership; they are different and complimentary, those characteristics and capabilities either for the organization, or for the individual marketer – although both are linked intimately and synergistically.

We need to truly undertake a 'Copernican' shift in marketing – we still talk about 'market' and 'customer' centricity but do not know how to be oriented as such; likewise we do not know – or at least we act as if we did not know – the difference between the *attainment* of sales and the *achievement* of health and enjoyment. Copernicus offered an alternative view that the earth revolved around the sun. Most of course, thought otherwise, that the sun was in motion around the earth. We can laugh about that now, in our gloriously modern age, but we *still* have our own equivalent of the earth-centric view – the company-centric perspective and locus – and have a very long way to go to realize the perfect and elegant customer-centric perspective and a more effective delivery orientation!

Addressing and realizing the options offered in this book is correspondingly taking a major step towards leadership; personal, as well as organizational leadership. We must be more assertive with our peers and adopt aggressive listening in the market to have any hope of attaining a fuller level of personal and organizational leadership, and become an exemplar of good marketing practice.

> *Strangely, most companies tend to focus on the acquisition of new business at the expense of increasing throughput to existing customers. And bizarrely they know they do it!*
>
> **DAVID JAMES HOOD**

Coercive power, whether mistakenly or wrongfully used in marketing in terms of pushing the proposition, or indeed in the way that we run organizations as some non-human entity, cannot be a good thing for commerce and society and we need to push for change to create a situation altogether more virtuous.

That is why there are common themes throughout this book that tackled together, can lead us towards the creation of a more virtuous discipline and profession. We need to redress and re-evaluate the important issues – the fact that we are now living in a knowledge-based world (was it any different beforehand? But at least we have a little more than tacit recognition that we do need *real* knowledge – good knowledge, free from all the clutter that those constraints can cause us to fret over) – to lead our companies and organizations to a sustainable healthy future.

To that end, the final conflict we examine is that of the *acquisition of sales* as a prime driver, raging against our desire to accumulate and apply knowledge to improve lives, experiences and profit for the customer, and better experiences and enjoyment for the consumer.

The resolution may not rely on forcing the conflict demonstrated in Figure 15 down one path rather than the other, but may accommodate both sides; but it does help us articulate, test and deal with one of the major conceptual limitations preventing us from achieving excellence and leadership in marketing.

Ultimately, the rewards of true marketing should be major competitive advantages and when deployed well, a firm and lasting profit swing. No less.

Marketing is supposedly worth three times more than any other business activity. Let us grasp the helm of the organization and prove that the marketer and marketing is up to the job, constantly and consistently.

FIGURE 15   Leadership in marketing: taking the strategic high-ground

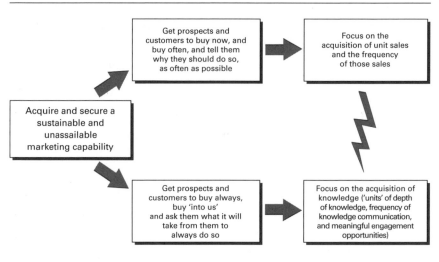

© David J Hood
The Marketing Manifesto™

Testing assumptions

1 **Get prospects and customers to buy now, and buy often, and tell them why they should do so, as often as possible, because:**

    a otherwise, they just will not buy of course!;

    b our competitors are doing the same, and we need to be sending out as many messages to the same people as our competitors, or more if possible;

c it is the kind of activity that is expected of us as marketers or as a high profile or aspirational company (the markets must be made aware of our organization and its propositions);

d we must get the maximum traction from any products or services we provide before they either get replaced or the customer or consumer switches to another provider and proposition, or our propositions become jaded or obsolete.

2 Therefore... focus on the acquisition of unit sales and the frequency of those sales, because:

a we constantly need to build and retain market share in terms of unit sales and frequency of sales transactions;

b markets constantly perish or are transient; so we need to 'milk them and leave' or redefine the market on our terms, whilst it lasts;

c we need to meet the pressures of short-term targets, which are always based on unit sales;

d it is easier to predict and manage sales (income-based projections about 'how many' and 'how often') using units (such as SKUs – stock-keeping unit) and multiple/frequency calculations (the so-called 'lifetime value');

e we can tinker with the proposition to suit and this is not too hard nor too costly, and doing this will always make it easy to attract and gain more custom.

3 Get customers and prospects to buy always, buy into us and ask them what it will take for them to always do so, because:

a 'buying always' from us involves taking a new approach and redefining 'lifetime value' of not only the customer or consumer, but *their* perception of value from and of *us*;

b we need to show more effective sincerity; to demonstrate in terms of specific actions that we truly care for the consumer, customer or prospect and ensure that loyalty *goes both ways*;

c we need to make sure that the consumer or customer sticks with us through good times and bad;

d we can respond with adequate speed and precision to their needs;

e it cuts out waste, reduces risk and inherently makes commercial sense.

4 Therefore... focus on the acquisition of knowledge, because:

a we have a standardized constant and consistent system to identify intellectual property (knowledge created or acquired from customer-need definition, blended with our own explicit and unique innovation processes and resulting 'smarts') that we can readily translate and transcribe into profitable propositions;

b we will meet the changing needs of the customer better if we are more informed about them, and the relationship is based on knowledge, human-to-human contact, aspirations and cooperation, and not based on the number or frequency of transactions;

c profitability is most assuredly based on knowledge in our brave new and exciting world that is the 'knowledge economy';

d strategic direction, tactical variance, products and service options and marketing mixes are best based on firm intelligence and our corporate and individual ability to learn and innovate accordingly is directly related to this ability and the power of potent intelligence; this manifests itself as enhanced brand equity, sustainable competitive advantage, high levels of goodwill and corresponding health and longevity for the business; and which collectively reminds us why we exist as marketers or organizations – to *understand* things and help people and other organizations as much as we can, not to sell as much as possible.

Core conflict

The conflict in Figure 15 runs deep – it is related to a number of other conflicts articulated in this book and to another major conflict that is

'selling to more customers versus selling to the same, existing customers'. From a quick glance at the conflict you can see why we are
forced down the route to **obsessing about new customers rather than
excelling at servicing existing ones** – if we find ourselves measured
and valued (both as an organization and as an individual) on unit
sales and frequency of sales, then new custom is our number one
priority when it comes to income generation.

> *Marketing is everything you do up to the close of the sale
> and everything you do after the sale to keep your customer
> coming back.*

DAVID KIMBALL

Couple this with what was said earlier about cost reduction and
removal being our internal focus and additionally wishing to deliver
less to the customer or consumer, then this is truly an unholy alliance
of the most self-destructive elements in business! Unsurprisingly
we swerve towards new sales from new customers, although we all
know the old adage that it is far more costly to go for new sales to
new customers than to existing customers!

What to CHANGE

- The disparate, fragmented corporate structures and associated
  introspective hierarchy that stifles effectiveness.

- A competitor-following, 'me-too' approach: following
  the vagaries and pressing 'initiative or imitation of the
  moment'; the fads and the fashions of the 'next best thing'
  to improve or to simply be seen to keep up with the
  competition.

- Create a process where definable, sustainable, and readily
  deliverable competitive advantage exists, at all times.

- The idea that value, longevity for the business and a
  measurement of customer satisfaction and value is generated
  simply by 'moving matter around'.

- The lack of a firm goal for the so-called 'business ecosystem'.

What to change TO

- A systemic marketing model to improve, maintain and create a constant flourish – **a definitive and elegant 'eureka moment' – for the value chain** (but make sure that we actually create and apply a systemic marketing model. We may wrongly assume that we have such a model, that we 'know our system' and are optimizing it; but perversely we may actually only be harming it as we invariably only deal with the parts that we know well or think we can or should affect. And it is probably the *wrong* part!).

- Own the genuine standard by which competitors in your industry or segment must match.

- Employ a *process-based marketing management (PBM²)* system and ethos and couple with pan-company marketing.

- A realization that it is *people* who are the source of 'competitive advantage knowledge' – remembering that knowledge is just not some isolated, codified ethereal substance and dealing with that fact accordingly.

- Acquiring a unique goal and purpose that reflects a fully shared understanding of the means by which the organization creates, delivers and grows *true* value.

HOW to change

- Use a Customer/Value/Intellectual Property (CVIP) funnel rather than a sales funnel (and conduct a full audit and keep an IP Asset Register updated with ongoing audit and input); and remove unit and frequency of sale as *the* measurement of success.

- Create a truly unique *means* to develop a USP (not just a unique selling proposition in itself, as a USP usually is somewhat perishable!). Again, we are working on this important facet of marketing. We intend to bring out definitive processes for developing 'USPs' – *that can give you the means to develop a real and continuing advantage*, not just the one-off and perishable 'USP'.

- Transform marketing from existing outdated, stagnant departmental structures to a horizontal and more inclusive process. *Strangely, when one looks at a series of marketing activities it usually starts off with a marketing process (marketing research) and ends up with a process (soliciting customer feedback) but isn't seen as a process to manage many of the component business activities in between.*

- Map engagement with all stakeholders – especially with employees (the latter must not only be through 'command and control' structures!). **It is not about commanding the resource – it is about aligning it with the market.** *Wow* – reminding ourselves again of the obvious; bizarrely for marketers we are not living up to our fundamental tenet!

- Bring marketing into every area of the business – get everyone involved and feeding into the PBM^2 system, teach them all about marketing and bring customer or consumer experience to them *all*; every member of your staff and colleagues, and get them to 'experience' the product and service and somehow let them *actually see and hear your prospects, consumers or customers.*

Leaders can conceive and articulate goals that lift people out of their petty preoccupations and unite them in pursuit of objectives worthy of their best efforts.

JOHN GARDNER

Reflection and action

We need to bring our colleagues along with us on the journey; let us face it, we are *marketers* so we should be able to promote *internally* to engage with and energize them. Top-level management, shareholders and partners also need to buy in to marketers and what marketing is all about, what it needs to be, and how it will *keep us all in jobs and making money.*

We need to see 'failure' in a different light – whether it be a stratagem, tactic, tweak, or result that we hadn't anticipated and didn't give us the immediate result desired; it should be welcomed – nay, embraced – not as a failure at all but as successful marketing research! Any engineer will tell you that there is no such thing as failure – all attempts at most actions will yield a result. Something positive can be taken from any activity or output; sometimes we just don't have the intuition, insight or means to gauge and measure it or place it in a useful context, that's all. We just need a more robust framework to give us increased precision at the input side of the equation, and an exceptional new marketing process and perhaps some not-yet-invented technology to create that evolutionary marketing and customer-centric organization that we aspire to be, or indeed would wish to lead.

We also need to redefine success – and see that quite differently too. Success is based on our integrity as marketers and organizations; our ability to leverage our joint capabilities to hone insights and responses to the core challenges and opportunities for the people who make up our markets. In this book, I hope that I have given sufficient building blocks that may lead to an overhaul of what success means – to marketing and to you.

We must **elevate the marketing process and subordinate all others to it**, and exalt the resulting process and marketing's more appropriate 'good corporate governance' measurements as *pre-eminent*; as organizations are complex and have too many conflicting measurements and gravitational pulls to work properly otherwise.

The purpose of marketing is the marketing of purpose.
DAVID JAMES HOOD

FINAL THOUGHTS

True leaders actually lead mindsets and perspectives, not companies or people. In providing leadership personally within your organization as a 'champion of the true marketing way', or an organization aspiring to become an exemplar of customer centricity, concentrate on the purpose; back it all up with customer or consumer and prospect insights, leverage your good personal standing (or improve it) within the organization, and lead them all on to a virtuous path of sustainable competitiveness and systemic value to society.

Agility is what the organization needs, and we need it to be able to meet the ever-changing and quicker-changing needs of the customer or consumer. Give the marketer the reins – through a true marketing sensing and respond process that **everything subordinates to**.

Give us the authority as well as the responsibility for resourcing up the organization to meet its current and future commercial and competitive requirements.

Ask yourself – am I, as a marketer or manager, ready to take that authority to lead, as well as grasping ownership of the tactical responsibilities for generating income for the business? Are you going to stretch yourself in these difficult and challenging times, taking hold of the reins of your own role and potential and steer your career path towards realizing what you intended for your life as a marketer or manager who enjoys the challenges of developing new innovations for the company and its markets?

I uphold that in the marketing position you currently have a major and yet probably unrealized role to play in the organization. Likewise, this book has advocated that marketing has not yet raised itself to the giddy heights that await it. The road ahead is not easy. But, the alternative is at best mind-numbing tediousness and at worst, finding yourself in a stagnant role or situation that in hindsight you could have avoided and the knowledge that a real opportunity for change was not grasped. Can you provide the marketing-leadership model for the organization and yourself that is so badly needed? Can you stretch and emancipate your organization and market as the principles of marketing would hold that you do? Can you use these conflict/constraints/dilemma methodologies to deliver an insight into your markets' needs (as well as your own) giving an evidential priority to modifications to the proposition – the marketing mix – and subsequently to your colleagues and management in confidence?

> *"Many people think of knowledge as money. They would like knowledge, but do not want to face the perseverance and self-denial that goes into the acquisition of it."*

> **JOHN MORELY**

What to do next? Test those conflicts and see what emanates from your own assessment of the conflicts and your own context; find illumination from your own knowledge, intuition and that context by **resolving your own core conflicts**. Follow the developing debates and discussions within Global Marketing Network and The Marketing Manifesto™, and continue to focus on the priority challenges and opportunities for marketing and the marketer. (See the resource section in the following pages).

Following on from this book, we are introducing the means for marketers to prioritize strategic and tactical change options:

- **Strategy**: what any change is for and precisely what and where it should be made at any one time; and why it is evidentially better than other options for change.

- **Tactics**: what form the change within the process, by which we provide and improve upon our product and service propositions, should actually take; and which subsequently gives marketers the means to predict changes accurately, and apply those tactics and appropriately measure that change.

Embrace a fulfilling and rewarding life as a marketer, within an organization that is exceptionally effective. **Join with the real agenda in marketing – that of resolving the key issues and opportunities for the marketer.**

We have lost our way; a few years ago I said, at the start of the new 'e-marketing' and 'e-everything' bubble, that we were in danger of 'delegating, relegating, and abdicating responsibility for modern market-ing to others' such as the ICT (information and communications technology) profession. The technologies and the cult of all things 'new' have certainly taken much away from the realm of the marketer – and now is the time for us to recapture it all within a marketing framework and process – whilst being comprehensively more inclusive about what marketing is and involving more of our colleagues who actually and identifiably, have an important marketing role.

The redistribution of marketing activities away from the marketer – and the fact that many marketing activities are traditionally not seen as such – may have affected our ability to perfect and control it to date. However, the upside of this is that marketing, through ICT and associated new technologies has arguably started to make its way out of the marketing functional silo already and is poised in a vacuum, ready for suitably firm and capable hands to better manage it.

Join Global Marketing Network, enjoy the various products, services and knowledge that are being cultivated as a result of the **evidential important needs of the marketer**; some of which are of course identified and clarified as mini-manifestos in this book. Rest assured, the resources developed and provided for you are critical to your performance and prowess as a marketer and your organ-ization's competitive capabilities. Keep engaging with me and Global Marketing Network, and keep following our tweets... or whatever takes the place of twitter, in time! Oh, the joys and challenges of continuous change...

> *Grasp and address, at long last, the choices proffered in these manifestos and liberate yourself from the frenzied conventions of the new and the fossilized chains of the past...*

Read it, Live it, Lead it.

DAVID JAMES HOOD

ACTION

Where do we go from here?

I trust that you have found *The Marketing Manifesto* thought provoking and may it have given you the basis of a rational foundation to inspire you to change your thinking about the 'marketer's world'. I also hope that you will in turn test your own assumptions and experiences about marketing within your own organization and choice of career path (whether you are a marketer or not) and hope it may help you and your organization succeed in whatever way you judge success.

The undercurrent in this book, unsurprisingly and perhaps even reassuringly, is that the consumer, customer or prospect is vital to all that we do. We badly need to resist the all-too-dominant current temptation to move further and further away from them, putting every barrier or surrogate gateway in the way of human-to-human, brain-to-brain marketing. To that end, I have included some resources at the end of this book that I think may help you head in the right direction. **These resources, and using the 'how to' sections of this book reinforced with your own assumption tests should put you on a path to greater engagement with your market.** In addition indeed, it should encourage greater engagement from the market towards you. We should move immediately from a push to a pull paradigm – the prospect, customer or consumer should have the best reason to purchase from you rather than another organization – because we can excel at how we do things with them rather than just what we do to them. I challenge you to continue to test your own assumptions, develop the themes contained within this book, engage with your colleagues and challenge and debate about what marketing means to them all and what it can do for them. Whatever definition you use for marketing, it starts and ends with the customer. The marketer needs redefining, his or her context is constantly being eroded, redefined and overtaken by events, and we need to badly redress that balance and take a leadership position within our organization and within business as a whole. We can only do this through adopting processes and roles that give marketing – and us – an unassailable position in the system and organization and redress some overdue issues.

Appendices

Appendices

GLOBAL MARKETING NETWORK

Global Marketing Network
When we talk marketing, we _really_ mean business

About Global Marketing Network

Global Marketing Network (GMN) is the Global Accreditation Body for Marketing Professionals. Global Marketing Network's vision is for a strong, unified and respected Marketing Profession, worldwide, achieved through the raising of standards within it.

It achieves this in collaboration with both organizations and individuals who share its commitment to and enthusiasm for that now widely-shared vision.

GMN achieves this through four key strategic programmes:

- Realizing the aspirations of Marketing Professionals worldwide – by recognizing and rewarding educational and professional achievements through awarding GMN Global Accreditation to individuals who satisfy GMN professional membership entry criteria, as assessed by the GMN Membership Committee against globally established standards of practice;

- Raising standards in marketing practice – by helping businesses achieve greater profitability and return on investment through a relentless focus, in all that we do, on what actually matters to people in business in the 21st century, through the design and development of global certification programmes, executive education and conferences, delivered through an international network of accredited delivery partners;

- Putting Marketing Professionals back in the Boardroom - by enabling employers to insist on and recruit the best and most up-to-date Marketing Professionals with the introduction of GMN's global Continuing Professional Development (CPD) Scheme and by identifying those Marketing Professionals who are Globally Accredited by profiling them in the GMN Membership Directory – only accessible on the official GMN website;

- Supporting today's Marketing Professionals around the world by enabling them to be more knowledgeable, capable and better networked, leading to improved employability, promote-ability and, ultimately, rewards – wherever they live and work in the world – through the GMN Online Community, collaborating with business schools and national professional associations, and endorsing and accrediting events and conferences.

GMN is the only worldwide body dedicated to raising standards in the Marketing Profession and to delivering a wider vision, developed with the most senior people in the profession. Worldwide, there is no other Global Accreditation Body for the Marketing Profession.

For more information please visit www.gmnhome.com

BOOK PARTNER-SPONSOR

 Microsoft Dynamics CRM

http://crm.dynamics.com

Microsoft, the world's largest software company, is placing itself and its sizable resources fully behind the marketer and marketing.

Its CRM Dynamics product has been evolving over recent years, to not only become a major Customer Relationship Management tool, but to quickly and now effectively offer both a 'premises' and online version of the product and one that has some marked 'XRM' platform capabilities and extensions to the product to increase functionality and productivity for the marketer.

Microsoft Dynamics Marketing Manager Louise Watkins said 'we are delighted to sponsor David's *The Marketing Manifesto*. This is a fantastic and MUST-read for marketers across the globe looking for inspiration amidst these tough times when apathy kicks in due to sheer volume of workload, pressure and less than pleasing results – despite our determined efforts. We have and still are weathering one of the most dramatic changes in businesses we have had to endure in our careers. *The Marketing Manifesto* casts a huge ray of hope and glimmers of new opportunity for us all in its clever and insightful chapters – directing, channelling and transforming our efforts to succeed in what now seems the intangible. Let's get back to basics; drive our profession to new heights; change the course of our profession beyond recognition – achieving what seems the impossible but is destined for greatness.'

Author of *The Marketing Manifesto*, David James Hood, welcomed both Microsoft's support for the book and for aligning themselves firmly with the marketing profession. Hood said 'It is great when such a major player in a sector looks to truly align itself with a community of practising professionals; in this case managers and marketers with a responsibility to bring in income for the organization. Microsoft is well known for making business software to help companies run more efficiently, now it seeks to additionally help businesses make money effectively.'

PARTNERS AND RESOURCES

www.theepsilonproject.com

The Epsilon Project™ is an important new cause and ongoing initiative to develop and bring to the marketer definitive and robust campaign management and proposition optimization capabilities, optimizing and reducing the many variables of the marketing mix. Simply subscribe to the initiative to keep abreast of all developments as they happen. Simplify marketing; get products, services and campaigns right as early as possible. Reduce the noise. Make better decisions.

www.twitter.com/projectepsilon

www.themarketingmanifesto.com

The Marketing Manifesto™ (Kindle version available on Amazon) – if you would like to follow further developments on the subjects covered in this book and receive updates from *The Marketing Manifesto*™ simply subscribe to follow the twitter feed at **www.twitter.com/themmanifesto**.

If you are interested in being alerted to the Author's future publications and appearances, simply subscribe to his personal tweets at: **www.twitter.com/davidhood**.

Additional related and relevant links and resources will be added or modified where and when appropriate.

CORPORATE CONVERSATIONS WITH DAVID HOOD

David James Hood PgDIM PgDED PGMN

The author, David James Hood, is available for speaking engagements, internal workshops or 'corporate conversations' about enhanced competitiveness for your organization. He would welcome a discussion about your own situation, objectives and challenges and how you can best grasp the opportunities advocated in this book.

David is a Professional Member (PGMN), a member of the advisory panel for GMN, and is also its CPD Director.

To contact David, simply visit: **www.davidjameshood.com** or **http://ie.linkedin.com/in/davidjameshood**. For 'Corporate Conversation' enquiries, email **davidh@mymarketinglife.com**.

WORKING WITH CORE CONFLICTS

The core conflicts offered in this book are the result of considered, deep cause-and-effect studies of the primary real-world problems and opportunities for marketing and the marketer.

You are encouraged to examine these conflicts and see if and how they are observed and discernible within your own context; the following worksheets will help you in this process.

When using the Core Conflicts, please read like this:
If we (main box) then we *really* need to (following box) due to the fact that (list the assumptions – those offered in the book's manifestos and add some of your own). Therefore, we *really* need to (final box) because of (the next set of assumptions).

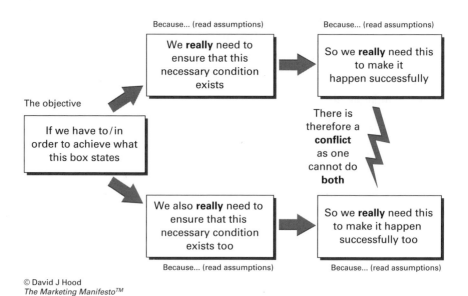

Because... (read assumptions)

We **really** need to ensure that this necessary condition exists

Because... (read assumptions)

So we **really** need this to make it happen successfully

The objective

If we have to/in order to achieve what this box states

There is therefore a **conflict** as one cannot do **both**

We also **really** need to ensure that this necessary condition exists too

So we **really** need this to make it happen successfully too

Because... (read assumptions)

Because... (read assumptions)

© David J Hood
The Marketing Manifesto™

Reading both top and bottom options really helps the reader to test the conflict, the underlying assumptions and in many cases come up with a strong and startling solution to break the conflict; such as a preferred or obvious route one way or the other or a solution that suits **both** necessary conditions that underpin the main objective or goal.

In life, very often the resolution to challenges and opportunities that confront us is 'almost there'. The underlying conflicts we find in marketing and business life, such as those articulated in this book, prevent us from resolving real problems – which **ultimately and invariably lead us to make wholly unwarranted compromises.** It is clearly seen that if one establishes that the core conflict results in the choice between two separate and diametrically opposing options or actions, and both cannot be undertaken simultaneously, then we are perhaps forced down one route over another; or otherwise compromise – so that the conflict and therefore the underlying problem **remains unresolved** or an opportunity left **unrealized.** Reading those Conflicts enables us to see clearly why we go down a given path, as both conditions stated immediately to the right of the main box (the goal or objective) are necessary. BUT – we are attempting to *resolve* the conflict: although we need both 'conditions' to apply, one 'route' is actually taking precedence, so this leads to continued conflict, unresolved issues and a plethora of undesirable knock-on effects which then subsequently manifest themselves as day-to-day fire fighting episodes that seriously undermine competitive performance. Assessing these and your own assumptions, testing them, breaking them; and then introducing new policies, thoughts, processes, or some other deliberate and breakthrough interventions into those conflicts can and usually does negate one or more of the major assumptions and leads to a **true and elegant breakthrough.**

...A 'eureka moment' indeed.

More on the use of clouds and conflicts

The creator of the cloud/core conflict/thinking processes – Eli Goldratt – outlines the use of these methods in online videos that can be purchased:

- **The Cloud Process/Thinking Processes** (this relates to people management but sets out their use as tools)
  www.mymarketinglife.com/cloud

- **Using Clouds/Conflict Analyses in Marketing**
  www.mymarketinglife.com/gm

WORKSHEETS

Updated versions of these and other simple worksheets are available to those who purchased this book and subscribe to The Marketing Manifesto website (*photocopy these, make your own, or download*).

Manifesto Worksheet

My notes on Manifesto or conflict:
How does it chime with my situation/context/problem?
What I need to change:
What I need to change TO:
HOW I will effect change:

Testing Assumptions

Key assumptions (copy table for each group of the four assumptions)
Do I have a breakthrough resolution to the core conflict that enables me to go down one preferred route? Write it here.
Do I have a breakthrough resolution to the core conflict that allows me to realize BOTH main necessary conditions to meet the objective articulated in the conflict? Write it here.

Notes Worksheet

Things I need to investigate further:
What is a one-line, simple summary description of my breakthrough ideas, so that I can describe it to all my colleagues?
What resources will I secure to make it all happen?
Links, references and contact details for the resources I will need:

INDEX

NB: page numbers in *italic* indicate figures